CAMPAIGN 330

TSUSHIMA 1905

Death of a Russian Fleet

MARK LARDAS

ILLUSTRATED BY PETER DENNIS

Series editor Marcus Cowper

OSPREY PUBLISHING
Bloomsbury Publishing Plc

PO Box 883, Oxford, OX1 9PL, UK
Kemp House, Chawley Park, Oxford OX2 9PH, USA
Email: info@ospreypublishing.com

OSPREY is a trademark of Osprey Publishing, a division of
Bloomsbury Publishing Plc

A CIP catalogue record for this book is available from the British Library.

ISBN: PB: 978 1 4728 2683 1
            ePub: 978 1 4728 2684 8
            ePDF: 978 1 4728 2685 5
            XML: 978 1 4728 2682 4

20 21 22 23   10 9 8 7 6 5 4 3

Index by Sharon Redmayne
Typeset in Myriad Pro and Sabon
Maps by Bounford.com
3D BEVs by The Black Spot
Page layouts by PDQ Digital Media Solutions, Bungay, UK
Printed and bound in India by Replika Press Private Ltd.

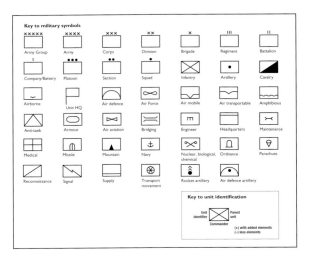

Key to military symbols

xxxxx	xxxx	xxx	xx	x	III	II
Army Group	Army	Corps	Division	Brigade	Regiment	Battalion
I	●●●	●●	●			
Company/Battery	Platoon	Section	Squad	Infantry	Artillery	Cavalry
Airborne	Unit HQ	Air defence	Air Force	Air mobile	Air transportable	Amphibious
Anti-tank	Armour	Air aviation	Bridging	Engineer	Headquarters	Maintenance
Medical	Missile	Mountain	Navy	Nuclear, biological, chemical	Ordnance	Parachute
Reconnaissance	Signal	Supply	Transport movement	Rocket artillery	Air defence artillery	

Key to unit identification

Unit identifier — Parent unit
Commander
(+) with added elements
(−) less elements

Artist's note

Readers may care to note that the original paintings from which the colour
plates in this book were prepared are available for private sale. All
reproduction copyright whatsoever is retained by the Publishers. All
enquiries should be addressed to:

Peter Dennis, Fieldhead, The Park, Mansfield, Notts, NG18 2AT, UK
Email: magie.h@ntlworld.com

The Publishers regret that they can enter into no correspondence upon
this matter.

Osprey Publishing supports the Woodland Trust, the UK's leading woodland
conservation charity. Between 2014 and 2018, our donations are being
spent on their Centenary Woods project in the UK.

To find out more about our authors and books, visit
www.ospreypublishing.com. Here you will find extracts, author
interviews, details of forthcoming events and the option to sign up for
our newsletter.

Author's acknowledgements

I would like to thank my older brother, George Lardas, for his assistance in
Russian translations. I would also like to thank Dennis G. Jarvis for allowing
me to use his photograph of the cruiser *Aurora*.

Author's dedication

I would like to dedicate this book to my sister-in-law Anne, the *matuska*
and another writer.

Illustration credits

The following abbreviations indicate the sources of the illustrations used in
this volume:
AC   Author's Collection
LOC   Library of Congress, Washington DC
SDASM   San Diego Air and Space Museum
USNHHC   United States Navy Heritage and History Command

Author's note on dates, time and names

Russia and Japan, the two combatants in the Russo-Japanese War, as well
as China and Korea, the two nations over whose soil and waters the battles
were fought, all used different calendars, which in themselves were
different from the Gregorian calendar used throughout much of the rest of
the world.

While Japan had adopted standard time zones, its ships set their clocks
to Tokyo time, two hours ahead of noon at Port Arthur. Russia had not yet
adopted standard time zones and would not until 1919. Its ships set noon
by the local time at their port of operation, Vladivostok or Port Arthur, or
set their clocks by local noon as they travelled, comparing it to St
Petersburg time.

Russia, Japan, China and Korea also all had different languages, none of
which used writing incorporating the Roman alphabet. The Russians used
the Cyrillic alphabet, while the three Asian nations used logograms. These
are transliterated to English using different methods. Additionally, all often
called places by different names. What the Chinese then called Lushun was
renamed Port Arthur by Russia and Ryojun City by Japan. Today it
is Lüshunkou.

Reducing the chaos this could create requires choices, and the following
were made in this book: All dates are given in the Gregorian calendar used
by the Western World at that time. Unless otherwise stated, all times are
given in Tokyo time, today's Japan Standard Time. Names of ships, people
and places use period names rather than current names. Chemulpo Bay is
today's Inchon, but the combatants called it Chemulpo. Consider it a
homage to the men who fought at these places. English transliteration of
the names also uses period methods, including use of now-supplanted
systems like Wade–Giles. For simplicity, Japanese and Russian names omit
diacritical marks (Togo not Tōgō). Japanese family names are placed first
(Uryu Sotokichi rather than Sotokichi Uryu as he was known at the US
Naval Academy).

Although the above choices may not be perfect, they are necessary
within the limitations of the Campaign series format.

CONTENTS

The strategic situation, 1904.

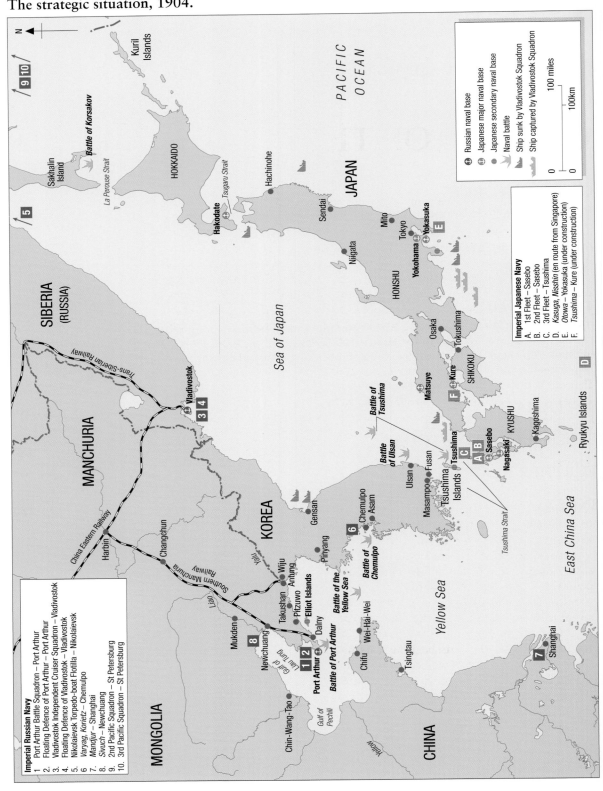

Imperial Russian Navy
1. Port Arthur Battle Squadron – Port Arthur
2. Floating Defence of Port Arthur – Port Arthur
3. Vladivostok Independent Cruiser Squadron – Vladivostok
4. Floating Defence of Vladivostok – Vladivostok
5. Nikolaievsk Torpedo-boat Flotilla – Nikolaievsk
6. *Varyag, Korietz* – Chemulpo
7. *Mandjur* – Shanghai
8. *Sivuch* – Newchuang
9. 2nd Pacific Squadron – St Petersburg
10. 3rd Pacific Squadron – St Petersburg

Imperial Japanese Navy
A. 1st Fleet – Sasebo
B. 2nd Fleet – Sasebo
C. 3rd Fleet – Tsushima
D. *Kasuga, Nisshin* (en route from Singapore)
E. *Otowa* – Yokasuka (under construction)
F. *Tsushima* – Kure (under construction)

Legend:
- Russian naval base
- Japanese major naval base
- Japanese secondary naval base
- Naval battle
- Ship sunk by Vladivostok Squadron
- Ship captured by Vladivostok Squadron

0   100 miles
0   100km

ORIGINS OF THE CAMPAIGN

The seeds for the Tsushima campaign were planted a decade before the May 1905 battle. By the late 19th century, the Eastern Asia kingdoms, including China, Korea and Siam, were adopting the new sciences and technologies offered by the European nations. No Asian nation pursued westernization more diligently than Japan, however.

More than any other Asian leader, Japan's ruler, the Emperor Meiji, realized unless his nation brought itself into the modern age his country would become a colony of a Western power. Between 1867, when he became emperor, and 1894, Meiji united Japan and modernized his nation, creating an industrial state to replace feudal Japan of the 1850s. Japan adopted Western-style legal and governmental systems and sent its brightest young minds to Europe and North America for education. It modelled its navy on that of the Royal Navy and its army on that of Imperial Germany, then the recognized leaders in their respective fields.

By 1894, Japan had enough confidence in its technology and military to fight its former overlord, China's Qing Empire. In less than nine months, Japan thrashed China. It wrested Korea from Chinese vassalage, gaining Taiwan, Penghu (the Pescadores Islands) and, temporarily, the Liaodong Peninsula as spoils of war.

Russia was Europe's most backward world power, technologically behind Great Britain, Germany and France. Its political and legal systems were even more primitive. Serfdom was abolished only in 1867, and in 1900 it was still a personal autocracy. Russia was large, however, and the easternmost major nation in Europe. Its military technology, primitive compared to that of Western Europe, was far superior to that of its eastern neighbours. As a result, it had swept through Central Asia and Siberia to reach the Pacific.

As Japan was defeating China in the 1894–95 First Sino-Japanese War, Russia was beginning its move south from Siberia, seeking a warm-water port: Vladivostok, Russia's major Pacific port, froze during winter. If Russia absorbed Manchuria, it would gain an excellent harbour at the southern tip of the Liaodong Peninsula for just such a port.

Japanese annexation of the Liaodong Peninsula threatened that plan. Russia convinced France and Germany, other European powers involved in colonial activities around China, to join forces and compel Japan

After the unification of Japan, many bright youngsters, including Togo Heihachiro, were sent overseas for training, to bring Japan into the modern world. Among them was Uryu Sotokichi, who commanded the 4th Division at Chemulpo Bay. He is pictured in his US Naval Academy midshipman's uniform in 1881. (USNHHC)

to disgorge the Liaodong Peninsula. Unwilling to fight three European powers simultaneously, Japan agreed to retrocede the Liaodong Peninsula in exchange for an increased war indemnity.

Two years after the retrocession, Russia occupied the Liaodong Peninsula, transforming the port city of Lushun into a naval base, its coveted ice-free Pacific port. In December 1897, Russia's fleet appeared off Lushun (renamed Port Arthur). In 1898, Russia leased the Liaodong Peninsula from China, and in 1899 began fortifying it.

Russia also began absorbing Manchuria into the Russian Empire. While now considered an integral part of China, in the 1890s Manchuria was seen as an obscure and distant Chinese frontier province. In addition to leasing the Liaodong Peninsula, Russia received concessions in other parts of Manchuria, and built railways through Manchuria, including one linking Vladivostok with the Trans-Siberian Railway. Japan wondered if the integration of Manchuria with Russia would lead to annexation.

Japan could endure that, especially as China continued unravelling. Japan and Russia cooperated during the 1900 international intervention triggered by the Boxer Rebellion. Russia contributed the most troops and resources and Japan the second greatest number of troops in putting down the anti-Christian, anti-foreign movement indigenous to China. Both nations consolidated positions in China.

It looked as if Russia did not plan to stop with Manchuria, however. In the late 19th century, Russia occupied Sakhalin Island just north of Japan's Hokkaido, despite Japanese claims of sovereignty. Russia also sought control over Korea. The latter emerged from the Sino-Japanese War a Japanese ally, but Russia was pushing in, attempting to implant a pro-Russian leader in Korea.

Japan could accept Russian domination or annexation of Manchuria, but not a Russian-dominated Korea. Korea was too close to the Japanese home islands for a hostile power to control. Starting in 1901, Japan began a series of actions to keep Korea friendly.

In 1902, Japan and Great Britain negotiated the Anglo-Japanese Alliance. Britain viewed Russia as a strategic threat, and wanted Japan as a counterweight. Japan disgorged the Liaodong Peninsula because it lacked the strength to fight multiple European nations simultaneously. A key provision in the alliance was that if either nation went to war, the other

Russia built the 1st Pacific Squadron to powerful levels in the years prior to 1904. Its home port was Port Arthur. This picture shows a September 1903 visit to Vladivostok. From left to right: *Sevastopol* (battleship), *Gromoboi* (rear, armoured cruiser), *Rossiya* (armoured cruiser), *Peresvyet* (battleship), *Bogatyr* (protected cruiser), *Boyarin* (centre, light cruiser), *Angara* (three funnels, black hull, transport), *Poltava* (battleship), *Petropavlovsk* (battleship). (USNHHC)

nation would join the war if a second nation declared war on the warring partner.

The alliance meant Russia could not go to war, even start a war with Japan, without involving Britain. If another nation allied itself with Russia, the latter and its ally faced war with the world's preeminent naval force – the Royal Navy. No European nation wanted a war with Britain unless absolutely necessary. The alliance assured Japan could fight Russia without risking repetition of the 1895 Russian-German-French combination, which forced the retrocession of the Liaodong Peninsula.

Japan still preferred avoiding war with Russia. In August 1903, she opened negotiations with Russia, hoping to set spheres of influence. Japan had no problems with Russian imperialism – provided that Russia excluded Japan from this.

Russia saw little reason to negotiate with Japan, despite impressive Japanese victories over China and Japan's remarkable technological progress. The Japanese were seen as uncultured barbarians, little different than the Aleuts or Ainu. Such Russian prejudice was fuelled by its leader, Tsar Nicholas II, and his cousin Kaiser Wilhelm II of Germany. Nicholas was ill-disposed towards Japan after surviving an assassination attempt by a Japanese policeman when visiting Japan as crown prince. Wilhelm, hoping to focus Russia's attention away from Europe, egged Nicholas on to eastern adventures. Wilhelm stoked fears of a 'Yellow Peril', expressing concern that the Chinese and Japanese, though inferior races, could threaten Europe.

The 1902 Anglo-Japanese Alliance was popular in both Britain and Japan. This cartoon celebrating the treaty appeared in *Punch*, a British humourous magazine of the era. (AC)

Russia stalled, yielding minor points, but refusing the Korean guarantees Japan desired. It also steadily built up its forces in Manchuria and the Pacific, sending its latest warships to Port Arthur. As Russia (and much of the world) saw things, it did not need to negotiate. It could take what it wanted from China, Korea and Japan, when it wanted, and was too powerful for any Oriental countries to oppose. Russia still desired a peaceful solution (favourable to itself, of course), but Japan became convinced Russia was stalling merely to gain time.

The Japanese realized time was against them. The Russians were completing the Trans-Siberian Railway. Only a gap across Lake Baikal remained. Once the gap was closed, Russia could pour endless troops and supplies across Russia all year round. It also continued to fortify Port Arthur and make gains in Korea. Japan was aware of the negative odds it was facing, but also believed if it did not stop Russia soon, Russia could easily gobble up Japan within the next 20 years. On 21 December 1903, Japan's cabinet decided war was the only course possible.

On 13 January 1904, the Japanese government sent Russia a best and final offer: Manchuria would be within Russia's sphere of influence, while Korea would be within Japan's. The Russian government simply ignored the proposal. On 4 February, Japan severed diplomatic relations with Russia. On 8 February, the Imperial Japanese Navy attacked the Russian Pacific Fleet at Port Arthur. Later that day, Japan declared war on Russia.

Russia reciprocated eight days later. By then, the two nations had been at war for over a week, the first major war of the 20th century. Both nations were heading towards a naval confrontation at the Tsushima Strait, the most decisive surface naval battle of a battle-filled century.

CHRONOLOGY

1894

21 November — Japan captures Port Arthur during the First Sino-Japanese War.

1895

17 April — Treaty of Shimonoseki ends the First Sino-Japanese War and cedes the Liaodong Peninsula to Japan.

23 April — Russia, France and Germany combine in the Triple Intervention to force Japan to return the Liaodong Peninsula to China.

11 November — Japan signs convention of retrocession returning the Liaodong Peninsula. Port Arthur is evacuated by December.

1897

1 December — Russian fleet arrives at Port Arthur on the Liaodong Peninsula.

1898

27 March — Russia leases the Liaodong Peninsula and Port Arthur from China.

1899

Russia begins fortifying Port Arthur.

1900

January–August — Japan joins the Eight-Nation Alliance intervening in the Boxer Rebellion in China.

1902

30 January — Japan and Britain sign the Anglo-Japanese Alliance.

1903

28 July — Japan opens negotiations with Russia to settle Manchurian and Korean issues between the two countries.

3 October — Russia sends a counter-proposal to Japan. Negotiations open between Russia and Japan.

1904

13 January — Japan sends a final offer to Russia.

6 February — Japan severs diplomatic ties with Russia.

8–9 February — Battle of Port Arthur: Japanese torpedo boats attack the Russian fleet at Port Arthur, and four hours later Japan declares war on Russia.

9 February — Battle of Chemulpo Bay.

9–14 February — Vladivostok Independent Cruiser Squadron conducts a commerce raiding sortie, sinking a Japanese transport.

13 February — Japanese fleet begins blockading Port Arthur.

13–14 February — Japanese fleet attempts to block the entrance to Port Arthur. The first attempt fails.

16 February	Russia declares war on Japan.
24 February	Vice Admiral Stepan Makarov is sent to Port Arthur to take command of the Russian Pacific Fleet, relieving Vice Admiral Oskar Stark.
24 February–1 March	Vladivostok Independent Cruiser Squadron conducts a further commerce raiding sortie.
9 March	Vice Admiral Makarov arrives at Port Arthur, and takes command of the Pacific Fleet.
26 March	Japan attempts to block the entrance to Port Arthur for a second time. The attempt fails.
1 April	Land siege of Port Arthur begins.
12 April	Russian fleet sorties from Port Arthur. *Petropavlovsk* and *Pobeda* strike mines returning. *Petropavlovsk* sinks; Vice Admiral Makarov is among the dead.
23–27 April	Vladivostok Independent Cruiser Squadron conducts a commerce raiding sortie, and ambushes a Japanese troop convoy sailing to Korea.
3–4 May	Japanese fleet attempts to block the entrance to Port Arthur for a third time, but fails.
15 May	Russian minefield sinks *Yashima* and *Hatsuse*.
12–19 June	On a further commerce raiding sortie, the Vladivostok Independent Cruiser Squadron sinks several Japanese troop transports in the Tsushima Strait.
23 June	Russian fleet attempts to break out of Port Arthur, but is forced back.
23 June–3 July	Vladivostok Independent Cruiser Squadron conducts a further commerce raiding sortie, and captures the British freighter *Cheltenham*.
17 July–3 August	On a further commerce raiding sortie, the Vladivostok Independent Cruiser Squadron sinks one British and one German cargo ship.
10 August	Battle of the Yellow Sea; the Russian Fleet at Port Arthur attempts to break out and form up with counterparts from Vladivostok.

Throughout most of the Russo-Japanese War, the Russian and Japanese navies fought on roughly equal terms. In 1904, the two navies fought several protracted battles, which damaged ships but failed to sink any. (LOC)

12 August	Vladivostok Independent Cruiser Squadron leaves Vladivostok to rendezvous with the Russian Port Arthur fleet.	**5 December**	Japanese Army captures 203 Metre Hill overlooking Port Arthur, allowing heavy artillery to bombard Russian ships in the harbour.
14 August	Japanese Second Fleet cruisers catch the Vladivostok Independent Cruiser Squadron returning to Vladivostok, sinking one and damaging two Russian cruisers.	**6 December**	*Poltava* is destroyed by bombardment from 203 Metre Hill.
		7 December	*Retvizan* is destroyed by bombardment from 203 Metre Hill.
20 August	Battle of Korsakov: *Novik* is scuttled.	**9 December**	*Pobeda*, *Peresvyet*, *Pallada* and *Bayan* are destroyed by bombardment from 203 Metre Hill.
15 October	Russian 2nd Pacific Squadron departs St Petersburg for Port Arthur.	**11–30 December**	*Sevastopol* moves out of range of guns on 203 Metre Hill, and is subject to a three-week attack by the Japanese Navy.
21 October	Dogger Bank Incident: Russian 2nd Pacific Squadron attacks British fishing boats, believing them to be shielding Japanese torpedo vessels.	**6 December**	Russian 2nd Pacific Squadron battleships reach Great Fish Bay, Angola.
26 October	Russian 2nd Pacific Squadron reaches Vigo, Spain.	**11 December**	Russian 2nd Pacific Squadron battleships reach Angra Pequena, in German South-West Africa.
3 November	Russian 2nd Pacific Squadron reaches Tangier, and splits into two parts: the battleships sail around the Cape of Good Hope, and the cruisers enter the Suez Canal.	**13 December**	*Takasago* strikes a Russian mine 37 nautical miles south of Port Arthur, and sinks.
16 November	Russian 2nd Pacific Squadron battleships reach Dakar, West Africa.	**29 December**	Russian 2nd Pacific Squadron battleships reach Île Sainte-Marie, Madagascar.
		1905	
26 November–1 December	Russian 2nd Pacific Squadron battleships reach Gabon and Libreville in western central Africa.	**2 January**	Port Arthur surrenders. *Sevastopol* is scuttled.

9 January	Russian 2nd Pacific Squadron reunites at Nosy Be off Madagascar; Vice Admiral Zinovy Rozhestvensky is ordered to wait there for the 3rd Pacific Squadron.	14 April–9 May	Russian 2nd Pacific Squadron is at Cam Ranh Bay in French Indochina.
		27–28 May	Battle of Tsushima.
February	President Theodore Roosevelt offers to mediate in the Russo-Japanese War.	7 July	Japan invades Sakhalin Island.
		31 July	Russians surrender on Sakhalin Island.
16 March	Russian 2nd Pacific Squadron departs Madagascar before the 3rd Pacific Squadron arrives.	8 August	Peace negotiations begin at Portsmouth, New Hampshire.
		5 September	Treaty of Portsmouth is signed, ending the Russo-Japanese War.
8 April	Russian 2nd Pacific Squadron reaches Singapore.		

Japanese destroyers from the 4th Destroyer Division make a night-time attack on Russian battleships at Tsushima. During the battle, they were armed with drifting mines. One set hit and sank the Russian battleship *Navarin*. (LOC)

OPPOSING COMMANDERS

Both the Imperial Japanese Navy and the Imperial Russian Navy had a cadre of trained, professional officers to lead their fleets and command their ships. The major officers on both sides had been trained at their nations' respective naval academies, or equivalent institutions in other countries. In both nations officers mastered the technical issues of running naval warships as well as combat. Several admirals even designed ships.

The major difference between the two officer corps lay in their heritage. Russia established its navy in the early 1600s and had three centuries of naval tradition and experience. Japan's navy did not exist before the unification of that nation in the late 1860s. Its first naval academy was established in 1871, and its first crop of graduates was just old enough to command fleets when the Russo-Japanese War began. In both nations, imperial favour played a role in promotion; however Japan's newness led to imperial favour being granted to officers demonstrating competence, while in Russia, family ties, loyalty and connections to the royal family were more important in determining this.

Togo Heihachiro fought his first battle at the age of 15, manning a cannon defending Kagoshima. After Japan's unification, he joined the navy and rose to command of the Combined Fleet in 1903. He became know as 'the Nelson of the East'. (USNHHC)

JAPANESE

Togo Heihachiro commanded the Imperial Japanese Navy Combined Fleet during the Russo-Japanese War. He was the architect of the Japanese naval strategy used during the war, and commanded the Combined Fleet at the Battle of Tsushima. Regarded as Japan's best naval commander, the contemporary Western press hailed Togo as the 'Nelson of the East' following the overwhelming Japanese victory at Tsushima.

Togo was born at Kagoshima on 27 January 1848, the third son of Togo Kichizaemon, a samurai. His first military experience was aged 15, when the Royal Navy bombarded Kagoshima in retaliation for the death of a British merchant. When the Satsuma Domain created a navy in 1868, Togo and two of his brothers joined. He was a junior officer aboard *Kasuga* during the Boshin War which united Japan, and saw combat at the Battle of Awa. When the Imperial Naval Academy was established in 1870, Togo was admitted.

One of 11 Japanese naval cadets sent to Britain for naval studies, Togo spent seven years training there and in the Royal Navy, including a circumnavigation as a sailor aboard HMS *Hampshire*. He returned to Japan in 1878 as a lieutenant, aboard *Hiei*, an ironclad corvette built for Japan in Britain. Given command of the steam sloop *Amagi* in 1884, Togo observed the French fleet during the 1884–85 Sino-French War from this vessel. He was promoted to captain in 1886, but spent three years ashore due to illness studying international and maritime law.

During the First Sino-Japanese War, Togo commanded the cruiser *Naniwa*. He sank a British-flagged transport carrying Chinese troops, but acted within international law, averting a conflict with Britain. He also commanded *Naniwa* at the Battle of the Yalu River.

Between the Sino-Japanese War and the Russo-Japanese War, Togo served as commandant of the Naval War College, commander of the Sasebo Naval College, and commander of the Combined Fleet. He was promoted to rear admiral in 1895 and vice admiral in 1898. Emperor Meiji gave Togo command of the Combined Fleet because he considered Togo fortunate.

Dewa Shigeto commanded the 3rd Cruiser Division throughout the Russo-Japanese War. He fought at Port Arthur, the Battle of the Yellow Sea and Tsushima. (USNHHC)

Togo proved fortunate during the Russo-Japanese War, achieving victory through equal measures of good judgement and good luck. Viewed as an average officer before the war, by its end he was considered one of the great admirals of naval history. His accomplishments were rewarded domestically and internationally. He received knighthoods or equivalents from seven European nations (including Russia).

In Japan, Togo was made Chief of the General Naval Staff, and raised to the peerage as a count. In 1913, he was promoted to marshal admiral (equivalent to admiral of the fleet), and between 1914 and 1924 he was in charge of educating Crown Prince Hirohito. Togo died on 30 May 1934 in Tokyo, Japan. The day before his death, he was elevated to the status of marquis.

Dewa Shigeto commanded the 3rd Cruiser Division of the Japanese fleet, a protected cruiser division, during most of the Russo-Japanese War. He took part in the Battle of Port Arthur, the Battle of the Yellow Sea and the Battle of Tsushima.

Dewa was born on 10 December 1856, in the Aizu Domain, to a samurai family. He attended the Imperial Naval Academy, graduating sixth out of 43 cadets in 1882. He was commissioned a sub-lieutenant in 1883, promoted to lieutenant in 1886, lieutenant-commander in 1890 and captain in 1894. During the First Sino-Japanese War of 1894–95, he served in home waters as a staff officer.

Promoted to rear admiral in 1900, he served as a cruiser division commander, remaining at sea through most of the Russo-Japanese War. His division contributed significantly to the Japanese victory at Tsushima. He was promoted to vice admiral in August 1904, and in December 1905 was appointed commander of the Third Fleet.

Dewa was elevated to the peerage in December 1907, when he was made a baron. He was promoted to full admiral in 1912. Because of his

Kamimura Hikonojo commanded the Second Fleet during 1904, with the assignment of stopping the Vladivostok Independent Squadron. Although he eventually ran them down at the Battle of Ulsan, he was heavily criticized for allowing them to raid Japanese transports. (AC)

reputation for integrity, in 1913 and 1914 he chaired the commission investigating procurement corruption. Dewa retired in 1925, and died in Tokyo on 27 January 1930.

Kamimura Hikonojo served as commander of the Second Fleet during the Russo-Japanese War. He was the victor at the Battle of Ulsan, and fought at the Battle of Tsushima, leading six armoured cruisers in the battle line.

Kamimura was born on 1 May 1849 in Kagoshima. He served as a soldier during the Boshin War, but transferred to the navy, entering the Imperial Naval Academy in 1871. Commissioned ensign in 1879, during the First Sino-Japanese War in 1894 he commanded the cruiser *Akitsushima*, winning distinction for his performance at the Battle of the Yalu River, afterwards being promoted to captain.

He served in a variety of roles after that war, rising to rear admiral in 1899 and vice admiral in 1903. When the Russo-Japanese War started, he commanded the Second Fleet, tasked with protecting the Sea of Japan. Initially he proved unable to contain the Vladivostok-based Russian cruiser squadron. He received heavy criticism after Russian cruisers sank several Japanese troopships. Later he defeated the Russian squadron in a battle off south-eastern Korea, and led the Second Fleet at Tsushima.

Kamimura commanded the Yokosuka Naval Base in 1905, was elevated to baron in 1907, and made a full admiral in 1910. He served on the Supreme War Council from 1911 until he retired in 1914. He died in Tokyo on 8 August 1916.

Kataoka Shichiro commanded the Third Fleet during the Russo-Japanese War. He fought with distinction at the Battle of the Yellow Sea and the Battle of Tsushima. He led the naval expedition during the invasion and capture of Sakhalin Island in the summer of 1905.

Kataoka was born on 12 January 1854 in Kagoshima to a samurai family. He entered the Imperial Naval Academy in 1871. Sent as an exchange student to Germany, he served aboard German warships, graduating with top honours. He became fluent in German, French and English. He was commissioned a lieutenant in 1881, served as an instructor at the Imperial Naval Academy, and returned to Germany for advanced studies in 1889, serving as naval attaché to Germany afterwards.

He served on the Imperial Japanese Naval Staff at the beginning of the First Sino-Japanese War, later commanding the corvette *Kongo* and cruiser

Uryu Sotokichi commanded the 4th Cruiser Division, with its protected cruisers, during the Russo-Japanese War. He was the victor at Chemulpo Bay and participated at Tsushima. (AC)

Naniwa. He was promoted to rear admiral in 1899 and vice admiral in 1903. His Russo-Japanese War command, the Third Fleet, consisted of warships too old or too worn out for service in the other two fleets.

He was elevated to baron in 1907, promoted to full admiral in 1910 and commanded the First Fleet from 1910 until retirement in 1911. He died in Tokyo on 11 January 1920.

Uryu Sotokichi served as commander of a cruiser division during the Russo-Japanese War. He commanded Japanese forces at the Battle of Chemulpo Bay, and commanded the 4th Cruiser Division during the Battle of Ulsan and the Battle of Tsushima.

Uryu was born to a samurai family on 2 January 1857 in Kanazawa, Kaga Domain. He entered the Imperial Naval Academy in 1871, but was transferred to the US Naval Academy in 1875, graduating in the class of 1881. He was commissioned a lieutenant in the Imperial Japanese Navy on his return, and spent the 1880s serving aboard various Japanese warships. From 1892 to 1896, he was naval attaché to France. He commanded the cruiser *Matsushima* upon his return. He was court-martialled after *Matsushima* collided with another cruiser, and jailed for three months. He later resumed command of *Matsushima*, and was promoted to rear admiral in 1900. He commanded the Japanese invasion forces at Chemulpo, defeating two Russian warships at the start of the Russo-Japanese War. He was promoted to vice admiral in June 1904.

He was elevated to baron in 1907 and made a full admiral in 1912. He served in the House of Peers in the Diet of Japan from 1922 to 1925, retired from the navy in 1927, and died on 11 November 1937 in Tokyo.

RUSSIAN

Zinovy Petrovich Rozhestvensky commanded the Imperial Russian Navy's 2nd Pacific Squadron sent from the Baltic Sea to reinforce Russian naval forces in the Pacific and relieve the 1st Pacific Squadron, trapped at Port Arthur. Upon the surrender of Port Arthur and Russian naval forces, Rozhestvensky, then in the Indian Ocean, was given command of all surviving Russian naval forces in the Pacific. This included the ships of the 3rd Pacific Squadron, then travelling to join him. He commanded the Russian Pacific Fleet, comprised of the combined 2nd and 3rd Pacific squadrons, at the Battle of Tsushima.

Rozhestvensky was born on 11 November 1848 in St Petersburg, Russia. His father was a St Petersburg physician. Joining the Imperial Russian Navy at 17, Rozhestvensky graduated from the Naval Cadet Corps (the Russian naval academy) in 1868 and the Mikhail Artillery Academy in 1873. Following commissioning, he served in the Baltic Fleet, transferring to the Black Sea Fleet in 1876.

During the Russo-Turkish War of 1877–78, Rozhestvensky commanded a torpedo boat and later an auxiliary cruiser, the gunboat *Vesta*. Commanding *Vesta*, Rozhestvensky fought a five-hour battle against the coastal battleship *Feth-i-Bulernd*. Although the battle was indecisive, Rozhestvensky's superior reported it as a victory, and Rozhestvensky was awarded the Order of St George.

Zinovy Rozhestvensky commanded the 2nd Pacific Squadron and the Russian Pacific Fleet at Tsushima. While an outstanding organizer, he was uncommunicative to subordinates and had an incandescent temper. He was known by the nickname of 'Mad Dog' (although never to his face). (AC)

Stepan Makarov was one of the outstanding admirals of any navy at the turn of the 20th century. His aggressive tactics could have pushed the Imperial Japanese Navy to breaking point if he had not died in combat so soon after his arrival. (AC)

After the Russo-Turkish War, Rozhestvensky was seconded to the Bulgarian Navy to help in its organization. He spent two years with the Bulgarian Navy before returning to Russian service, spending the period 1891–93 in London as Russian naval attaché to Great Britain. In 1894, he commanded the armoured cruiser *Vladimir Monomakh*, and the coastal defence ship *Pervenets* from 1896 to 1898.

In 1898, he was promoted to rear admiral, and given command of the Baltic Fleet's gunnery school. In 1900, after the coastal battleship *General Admiral Apraksin* ran aground, Rozhestvensky was given the task of salvaging it, which he completed successfully. He became chief naval aide to Tsar Nicholas II in 1902. The following year, Rozhestvensky became Chief of the Russian Naval Staff, the third-highest position in the Imperial Russian Navy.

In April 1904, he was given command of the 2nd Pacific Squadron, with the task of relieving the 1st Pacific Squadron, trapped in Port Arthur. Rozhestvensky picked the ships assigned to the squadron, chose the route and planned the logistics involved in its movement. He successfully completed this formidable logistical feat, but was met and defeated by a prepared Japanese fleet off Tsushima before reaching his goal of Vladivostok.

Rozhestvensky was seriously wounded early in the battle and later captured by the Japanese. Returned to Russia after the war, he was court-martialled and pled guilty to charges arising from the loss. He retired from the navy in 1906, and died in St Petersburg in January 1909.

Stepan Osipovich Makarov was born on 8 January 1849 in Nikolaev, a Russian Black Sea port. His father was a junior naval officer. Makarov entered the Nikolaev Naval Academy, preparing for a career in the merchant service, but at 15 transferred to the Imperial Russian Navy. As a naval cadet, Makarov sailed to San Francisco in a Pacific Fleet warship. He transferred to the Baltic Fleet in 1866. He published his first technical article in 1867 and created his first invention (an improved collision mat) in 1870. These were the first in a long series of publications and inventions he developed.

During the Russo-Turkish War of 1877–78, Makarov's innovative torpedo attack tactics gained combat success for his torpedo boat squadron. In 1890, he was promoted to rear admiral, the youngest ever, and in 1896 to vice admiral. Between 1880 and 1900, he published over 50 articles, designed several successful ships and modernized the Russian Navy.

Upon the outbreak of the Russo-Japanese War, Tsar Nicholas II assigned Makarov command of the Pacific Fleet. After arriving at Port Arthur on 8 March 1904, he began a training programme and instituted aggressive operations, making morale soar. On 13 April, while leading a sortie against the Japanese Navy, his flagship *Petropavlovsk* struck a mine and sank, killing Makarov and over 600 other members of its crew.

Wilgelm Karlovich Vitgeft was born in Odessa on 14 October 1847. He graduated from the Naval Cadet Corps in St Petersburg, Russia in 1868. He participated in the circumnavigation of the world aboard the clipper *Vsadnik* shortly after graduation. Thereafter he served in the Baltic Fleet from 1870 to 1899. He had a variety of seagoing and shore assignments during that period, being promoted to lieutenant in 1873, a captain of the second rank (equivalent to a commander in the US or Royal navies) in 1884, and a captain of the first rank in 1894, commanding the torpedo cruiser *Voyevoda*.

In 1899, he was promoted to rear admiral and transferred to the Pacific Fleet. He served as chief of the naval department under Viceroy for the Pacific, Admiral Yevgeny Alexeiev. This was an administrative position. After the Russo-Japanese War began, he was appointed Chief of the Naval Staff of the Supreme Commander in the Far East, a deputy to Admiral Makarov.

After Makarov's death on 13 April 1904, Vitgeft, as senior naval officer in Port Arthur, assumed command of the Pacific Fleet. Unlike the aggressive Makarov, Vitgeft believed in maintaining a 'fleet in being', using the Port Arthur fleet as a threat by its existence rather than risking it in battle. As the siege of Port Arthur continued, Alexeiev ordered Vitgeft to move the fleet to Vladivostok. Vitgeft attempted a breakout on 23 June, but returned to Port Arthur. He remained there until 13 August, when following a direct order from Alexeiev backed up by Tsar Nicholas II, he sortied from Port Arthur.

Despite Vitgeft's misgivings, the breakout almost succeeded. In the resulting Battle of the Yellow Sea, Vitgeft managed to outmanoeuvre the Japanese and had a clear route to Vladivostok by late afternoon. Then, at 6.40pm, less than an hour before sunset, Vitgeft's flagship was struck by two 12in. shells, one of which landed above the bridge, killing him and most of his staff. In the subsequent confusion, the fleet returned to Port Arthur or fled to neutral ports.

Nikolai Ivanovich Nebogatov was born on 20 April 1849 near St Petersburg, Russia. His father was a career naval officer. He became a naval cadet at 16, graduating in 1869, and served thereafter in the Baltic Fleet. His career progression was slow. He was promoted to lieutenant in 1874, to captain in 1894 and rear admiral in 1901. During that period he was steadily employed but in undistinguished positions. He received his first command in 1888, the gunboat *Groza*. He also commanded the gunboat *Grad*, and, during the 1890s, the cruisers *Krejs*, *Admiral Nakhimov* and *Minin*. His promotion to rear admiral came with appointment to command the naval artillery school, an admiral's assignment.

When the 3rd Pacific Squadron was formed, several more senior admirals turned down the command due to the obsolescence and unsuitability of the ships and the lack of trained crew. Nebogatov reluctantly accepted, and took the ships to join Rozhestvensky. When the 3rd Pacific Squadron caught up with Rozhestvensky's ships, the latter refused to speak to Nebogatov. Later Rozhestvensky did not inform Nebogatov of the death of Rear Admiral Dmitry von Folkersam, which made Nebogatov second in command of the Russian Fleet.

Nebogatov's squadron remained largely unengaged by the Japanese fleet on the first day of Tsushima, but was trapped on the second. By then, Nebogatov was in command of the entire fleet. Facing a situation where the Japanese ships were faster than and outranged the surviving Russian warships, Nebogatov surrendered the ships to preserve the lives of his crews. He was court-martialled in 1906 for improperly surrendering the fleet, found guilty and sentenced to death. The sentence was commuted to ten years, and Nebogatov was released in 1909. He died on 4 August 1922 in Moscow.

Nikolai Nebogatov had an undistinguished but competent career in the Imperial Russian Navy prior to the Russo-Japanese War. He reluctantly accepted command of the 3rd Pacific Squadron when others, more senior, refused. Command of the Russian Pacific Fleet fell to him near the end of the battle's first day. (AC)

OPPOSING FORCES

As the 20th century opened, fleets were armed with battleships, cruisers and torpedo vessels. The battleship of 1904–05 was a mixed-battery warship, armed with a main battery of two to four large guns (typically 10in. to 12in.), a secondary battery of medium-calibre guns (6in. to 9.2in.) and a set of quick-firing light guns (typically 50mm to 4.1in.). They also carried two to four torpedo tubes, usually in underwater mountings. The mixed heavy and medium guns were for use against other enemy battleships and cruisers. The quick-firing guns were intended to drive off torpedo vessels. Battleships displaced between 10,000 and 20,000 tons.

Three categories of cruisers existed: armoured, protected and scout. Armoured cruisers were miniature battleships. They carried heavy armour (although not as thick as battleships) and a main battery of 8in. guns. They carried a secondary battery of between six and 16 4in. to 6in. guns, between 10 and 16 quick-firing guns for torpedo boat protection and up to four torpedo tubes. Armoured cruisers displaced between 5,000 and 10,000 tons.

Protected cruisers had lighter armour. Some carried two to four 8in. guns, but most had a main battery of 4in. to 6in. guns as well as quick-firing guns

The typical battleship of 1904 had four 12in. guns in two turrets, one fore and one aft. It carried a secondary battery, usually of 6in. guns. The most modern battleships of that era carried these in wing turrets. Older battleships frequently used casemates along the sides. (USNHHC)

447,315 Tons 220,755 Tons 224,257 Tons 252,661 Tons

Russia. 1904 Japan. Russia. 1905 Japan.

Comparative Size of the Russian and Japanese Navies in 1904 and To-Day.

The comparative strengths of the Russian and Japanese navies at the start and the end of the Russo-Japanese War is starkly illustrated with this graphic, which appeared in a 1905 issue of *Scientific American* magazine. (AC)

and torpedo tubes. They were intended as fleet scouts, but were capable of participating in surface battles. Scout cruisers were unarmoured ships with a small battery of medium guns. Intended to conduct scouting and carry messages, they were a disappearing class by 1904. Radio appeared in the late 1890s, eliminating the need for ships to carry dispatches and for swarms of scout cruisers. Both sides still used these ships, although armed merchant cruisers could substitute for purpose-built scout cruisers. Displacement of protected and scout cruisers typically ranged between 1,000 and 7,000 tons.

The hottest weapon of the period was the torpedo – a self-propelled mine which struck underwater. It was a short-ranged weapon, but naval gunnery of the day was short, too. While battleships and cruisers carried torpedoes, these generally proved ineffective delivery systems. Purpose-built small vessels were built to carry and launch torpedoes.

Torpedo boats typically carried one or two torpedo tubes and displaced between 60 and 300 tons. Destroyers, or torpedo boat destroyers, were slightly larger – up to 500 tons – with two to four torpedo tubes and two to five quick-firing guns. While originally intended to hunt torpedo boats, destroyers also proved useful in delivering torpedo attacks. Submarines did exist in 1904, but were not used in the Russo-Japanese War.

Less glamorous than torpedoes, but ultimately deadlier, were stationary mines. A mature technology by 1904, they were widely used by both navies.

The navies of Japan and Russia appeared similar on paper, but were fundamentally different. Both navies obtained ships from foreign sources, purchasing warships and naval weapons such as artillery and torpedoes outside their country. Both countries were developing domestic shipbuilding industries capable of constructing state-of-the-art warships. By 1904, Russia was building vessels as large as battleships in its own dockyards. Japan was further behind, having only built cruisers in Japanese yards. Both nations still used ship designs developed in other European nations or the United States.

However, there were critical differences. Although Japan could not build ships as large as Russia could, the quality of ships built in Japanese yards was superior. Japan's repair facilities were also more efficient, especially in the Pacific. Indigenous Japanese munitions were the best in the world, superior to munitions manufactured in Russia.

The two navies appeared to man their ships in a similar manner. Common seamen, even in peacetime, were conscripts (this applied to most continental navies of the time). Conscripts were generally drawn from rural peasants, while volunteers were usually mariners or men interested in becoming mariners. Since Russia lacked a large merchant marine fleet and Japan had no oceangoing merchant vessels until after 1867, both navies had to use conscripts to satisfy manpower needs.

Even with this similarity, the two navies differed. Russian peasants served reluctantly. In Japan, the navy was seen as a high-tech career. Japanese farm boys saw the navy as a career alternative to farming, and volunteered for the navy in preference to the army.

THE IMPERIAL JAPANESE NAVY

The core of the Imperial Japanese Navy at the start of the Russo-Japanese War was six modern battleships and six modern armoured cruisers paid for by the spoils of the Sino-Japanese War of 1894–95 through the ten-year Naval Expansion programme. (AC)

The combat core of the Imperial Japanese Navy in 1904 consisted of six battleships, eight armoured cruisers (including two newly purchased before the war began), eight protected cruisers and nearly four dozen destroyers and torpedo boats. These were modern vessels: all had been built from 1892 onwards. Two protected cruisers were under construction in Japanese shipyards when the Russo-Japanese War started. Both saw service during the war, and fought at Tsushima.

In addition to these first-line vessels, Japan possessed 25 other warships when its armed merchant cruisers were included. These ranged from an older battleship and armoured cruiser captured from China during the First Sino-Japanese War, to ironclad corvettes built in the 1870s but still in service. Many could not serve in a line of battle, but still had utility as patrol vessels, pickets and convoy escorts. The fleet had a small but well-balanced train of repair ships, hospital ships, destroyer tenders and supply vessels.

Most of the Imperial Japanese Navy of 1904 had been built in foreign shipyards. All six Japanese battleships were built in Great Britain (the captured battleship had been built in Germany). Four of the armoured cruisers were built in Britain between 1896 and 1901, one in France and one in Germany. Just before the war started, Japan purchased two other armoured cruisers originally built in Italy for Argentina, but sold due to Argentinian financial problems. Japan outbid Russia for the vessels, which arrived after the war started.

Battleships and armoured cruisers were capital ships, the decisive vessels in naval battles. The limited ability of Japan to build its own capital ships, combined with the length of time it took to build capital ships meant it would fight a war with whatever vessels it had when the war began, with no replacements. Japan had two battleships on order in Great Britain, but due to neutrality laws they could not be delivered while Japan was a belligerent.

Japan started building its first capital ships during the Russo-Japanese War, the two ships of the Tsukuba class. The ships featured an armoured cruiser hull with battleship armament of four 12in. guns. A Japanese design, neither ship was completed during the Russo-Japanese War.

Japan also built smaller warships, up to and including protected cruisers. Over half of their cruising warships had been built in the Home Islands, and two-thirds of their modern protected cruisers were built domestically. Most of its commissioned destroyers and torpedo boats had been built in Europe, but in 1903 it had begun building in a major way, with 15 destroyers and nine torpedo boats under construction at Yokosuka, Kure and Kawasaki.

One area in which the Imperial Japanese Navy shone was in infrastructure. It had five naval shipyards with five dry docks, three large building slips and one dry dock under construction. Three of the existing dry docks and the one under construction could accommodate Japan's battleships. The one being built, when finished, was the world's largest. In addition, Japan had building yards for destroyers at Kobe and Yokasuka.

Japan had naval harbours at Nagasaki, Kobe, Kure, Sasebo, Matzuru, Takeshiki (in Tsushima) and Ominato. All were fortified. While Takeshiki Naval Base was a coaling station, the rest had repair facilities.

Japan's investment in maintenance facilities allowed it to repair any warship up to and including battleships. This included complete rebuilds. When *Mikasa*'s magazines exploded shortly after the war's end, the ship was returned to service, with its interior completely replaced.

Japan frequently made use of this capability during the war. The battleship *Asahi* struck a mine off Port Arthur in November 1904. Despite damage which almost sank it, *Asahi* was fully repaired by April 1905 and participated at Tsushima. Similarly, *Mikasa*, hit 20 times during the Battle of the Yellow Sea and with its aft 12in. turret knocked out of action, was back in service within a few months.

An additional Japanese advantage came in the form of logistics. Japan had stockpiled replacement parts, including barrels for its 12in. guns. By 1904, Japanese industry had matured. Japan lagged behind the west in production of armour plate, but would catch up by the end of the decade. Its technology may not have been as advanced as that of Britain or the United States, but it was equal or superior to that of Russia. It could produce much of its own munitions as well as its own ships. One technical advantage Japan had over Russia was its Shimose gunpowder. Developed domestically by naval engineer Shimose Masachika, it had greater explosive power than any other powder then used by the world's navies.

The Imperial Japanese Navy had a professional and competent complement of officers and men. The officers were overwhelmingly drawn from Samurai families, some 85 per cent. Applications to become line officers were made between the ages of 16 and 19. To be accepted, they had to pass a physical examination and a competitive academic examination. Only the top 15 per cent were accepted to the Imperial Japanese Naval Academy at Etajima. Engineering officers went to a separate college at Yokosuka.

Etajima cadets attended three years of classes and a final year aboard a training ship. Engineering cadets spent four years at Yokosuka. Both had to pass an examination to receive a commission. They had to retake any failed examination six months later. A second failure eliminated them.

Officers could be promoted from the lowest commissioned rank to the equivalent of lieutenant-commander after eight years' service. Subsequent promotion was based on performance through board reviews. Officers experienced 'up-or-out' promotions. A lieutenant had to retire at the age of 42 if not promoted.

The sailors used to man Japan's warships were drawn from Japan's lower classes, typically peasant farmers. All men were subject to conscription at age 20. If conscripted into the navy, the man served four years before being discharged. Men could also volunteer to serve a six-year term if they were between the ages of 17 and 21. All sailors had to pass a physical and demonstrate literacy and competence in basic mathematics.

However, there were relatively few conscripts because most of the manpower needs were filled by volunteers. Most volunteers came from Hokkaido or northern Honshu, areas with short growing seasons and low fertility. Young Japanese men viewed the high-tech navy as a way out of life on a small farm.

Both conscripts and volunteers could remain in the navy at the end of their terms. Many chose to do so, and remained until retirement age. They could also be promoted to petty officer and warrant officer positions aboard a ship. However, sailors, regardless of rank, were ineligible for officer commissions, and petty and warrant officers did not run watches. Sailors were pensioned off at age 40. Petty officers could remain in the navy until age 45, with warrant and senior warrant officers retiring at age 50 and 55, respectively.

In many ways, the 1904 Imperial Japanese Navy was like the United States Navy during the War of 1812 – a relatively new service, with first-rate ships. Its officers and crews were competent and experienced, with the officers rising to command positions having combat experience gained in earlier wars. Despite this, Japan was facing a much larger opponent. The odds were heavily against a Japanese victory, unless it received some lucky breaks. Louis Pasteur once said, 'Chance favours only the prepared mind.' And Japan was prepared.

THE IMPERIAL RUSSIAN NAVY

In 1904, Russia had the third largest navy in the world: 17 battleships, 12 armoured cruisers, 13 protected cruisers, 12 scout cruisers, 73 destroyers and nearly 200 torpedo boats. In addition, it could draw upon a large pool of

Russia's navy was much bigger than Japan's, but it was split into three widely separated parts. The Pacific Fleet was the biggest, and had the best ships and the most disciplined and experienced sailors. This shows an inspection aboard a Russian cruiser in Asian waters. (AC)

coastal defence ships, gunboats, armed merchant cruisers and superannuated battleships.

On paper, Russia's fleet was more than sufficient to crush the Imperial Japanese Navy. However, Russia's ships were divided into three geographically separated and roughly equal fleets: one in the Pacific, one in the Baltic Sea and one in the Black Sea. By sea, the Black Sea Fleet was nearly 10,000 nautical miles from Russia's major Pacific port (Port Arthur), while the Baltic Sea Fleet, if it took the Suez Canal, faced a voyage of 14,000 nautical miles. Around Africa it was over 18,000 nautical miles.

The geographical differences understated the problem, however. The Black Sea Fleet had to pass the narrow Turkish Straits to exit the Black Sea, and Turkey could deny passage to a belligerent. Russia also lacked coaling stations between its European and Pacific ports. During peacetime it could use foreign ports, but during wartime a warship of a belligerent nation could only spend 24 hours in a neutral port to refuel and re-provision before risking being interned until the end of the war. Any movement of ships from Europe to the Pacific would be a formidable undertaking once war was declared.

Yet the Russian Pacific Fleet by itself was superior to the Japanese fleet. It had seven battleships, all relatively modern (only the Baltic Fleet's newly commissioned and nearly finished Borodino-class battleships were newer). It also had nine armoured cruisers, two protected cruisers, 24 destroyers and 17 torpedo boats. There were also 20 other warships in the Pacific, typically different types of gunboats, larger than a destroyer but smaller than a protected cruiser.

The Russian Pacific force was weakened by geography. It was distributed between three Russian ports: Port Arthur on the Liaodong Peninsula, Vladivostok in southern Siberia and Nikolaievsk on the Amur River, across from the northern end of Sakhalin Island. The two main naval bases were Port Arthur and Vladivostok. Only torpedo boats were stationed at Nikolaievsk.

But Port Arthur and Vladivostok were separated by the Korean Peninsula. The only way to travel between them was through the Japanese-dominated Tsushima Strait, or to steam all the way around the Japanese Home Islands. Ships at one harbour could not support ships at the second. Russia solved that by stationing its major warships, including all of its battleships and all but four armoured cruisers, at Port Arthur.

A further handicap was a lack of shipbuilding facilities in the Far East. Like Japan, Russia was attempting to modernize and industrialize. It was further along than Japan, yet was still behind nations like Britain, France and Germany. While it was capable of building battleships within Russia, it could only build them in its European ports: St Petersburg in the Baltic, and Sevastopol and Nikolaev on the Black Sea. It was still using foreign naval architects to assist its domestic designs and was still purchasing major warships abroad as late as 1902, including the battleship *Tsesarevich* and the armoured cruiser *Bayan* from France.

It also had only limited repair capabilities at its Pacific ports. While its largest Pacific squadron was stationed in Port Arthur, its major Pacific repair facilities were in Vladivostok. Port Arthur had only one dry dock. It was 400ft long, large enough to take any of the battleships stationed there, but Port Arthur's repair facilities were limited. Russia had not been able to add many due to its short occupation of the port: the initial emphasis had been on fortification rather than infrastructure. Vladivostok had one 550ft dry dock and a 300ft floating dock as well as a pair of slips, but it was only capable of minor repairs.

Additionally, the shipwrights Russia did have in the Pacific were notoriously inefficient. Repairs were slipshod and progressed slowly. A moderately damaged ship, one Japan would have had ready for sea in a few months, would be out of action until the war's end.

Russia produced its own supplies, ammunition and parts for its navy. It was also the world's leader in mine warfare. It pioneered minelaying tactics, even building minelaying cruisers. But its Pacific Fleet was at the end of a long supply line. Everything had to be shipped from European Russia. Sea routes were unusable in wartime. Japan could blockade Port Arthur and Vladivostok.

The Trans-Siberian Railway was the only land link between European Russia and Vladivostok or Port Arthur, with the last third travelled along the China Eastern Railway and Southern Manchuria Railway in China. There was a gap around Lake Baikal in 1904, bridged by two ferries. The ferries could not run in winter, when the lake was frozen over, and instead cargo had to be transported by sledge around the lake. Over most of the route the railway was single track. Two-way traffic required coordination, which broke down when the railway was heavily loaded. Getting supplies east was a challenge, largely because of difficulties in bringing empty trains west against

In 1904, Russia was a world leader in mine warfare. It built the first cruisers designed as minelayers: *Amur* and *Yenisei*. The concept was widely copied, including by the Japanese. This shows *Yenisei* deploying mines through its stern doors. (AC)

the flow of traffic. Fortunately, Russia started the Russo-Japanese War with sufficient stocks of ammunition and supplies at Port Arthur and Vladivostok.

Russia's officer corps went through the same type of training as Japanese officers: attendance at a naval academy for three years followed by a year on a training ship for line officers. Only aristocrats or sons of naval officers were admitted. They passed an examination to enter the academies and a separate one to receive a commission, but these were not as rigorous as Japanese examinations. Additionally, officer candidates could skip the academies with permission from the Admiralty, if they passed the final examination. These officers were typically sent to unpopular postings, such as the Caspian Sea or the Siberian Fleet.

Officers were expected to go through further training, both in specialty areas such as gunnery, navigation or torpedoes, and in naval strategy. Promotion was based on sea service, with officers failing to get promotion being retired at different ages. Ensigns involuntarily retired at age 40; lieutenants at 47. The result was that the average age of Russian officers was higher than that of Japanese ones. Sea service was sought by the ambitious or given to those with no interest, service at shore postings being preferred.

Russia manned its navy using conscripts. Men were chosen by lot at age 21. If selected, they had to serve seven years. Unlike in Japan, sea service was unpopular: it meant leaving home, and sailors were not allowed to marry while on active duty. Sailors were further separated into military and civil branches. Military corresponded to a deck position – duties involving

Often unmotivated and frequently serving reluctantly, the Russian sailor would fight tenaciously – if fatalistically – when led properly. *Kniaz Suvorov* was the flagship of the 2nd Pacific Squadron. This is its crew posing before its departure. (AC)

seamanship or handling weapons. These men could be promoted to corporals (equivalent to petty officers) and conductors (equivalent to chief petty officers); the Imperial Russian Navy did not have warrant officers. Civil branch personnel served as stokers, engine-room personnel, sick bay attendants or yeomen. In some areas they could be promoted to a corporal, but in most they could expect no promotion.

The Russian sailor was older than his Japanese counterpart, less educated and less motivated. He generally had spent less time at sea and due to the incentive system (or lack of one) showed less initiative. Russia always was short of sailors, with the best ones being sent to the active fleets. At the start of the Russo-Japanese War, this was the Pacific Fleet.

The Imperial Russian Navy was not a bad navy, but not nearly as good as it thought it was. More importantly, it dangerously underestimated its most likely opponent, Japan. It could not imagine a non-European power fielding a competent navy. Three hundred successful years of fighting Asian nations left Russia with a dangerous blind spot. It was living on its reputation.

ORDERS OF BATTLE

Note: in the lists that follow, ships marked with an asterisk (*) were sunk or captured in battle.

THE IMPERIAL JAPANESE NAVY

COMBINED FLEET

Vice Admiral Togo Heihachiro (flagship *Mikasa*)

FIRST FLEET

Vice Admiral Togo Heihachiro (flagship *Mikasa*)
1st Division (Rear Admiral Nashiha Tokioki, flagship *Hatsuse*)
Battleships *Mikasa* (Mikasa class), *Asahi* (Asahi class), *Fuji* (Fuji class), *Yashima** (Fuji class), *Shikishima* (Shikishima class) and *Hatsuse** (Shikishima class)
Dispatch vessel *Tatsuta* (Tatsuta class)
3rd Division (Rear Admiral Dewa Shigeto, flagship *Chitose*)
Protected cruisers *Chitose* (Chitose class), *Takasago** (Takasago class), *Kasagi* (Chitose class), *Yoshino** (Yoshino class)
1st Destroyer Division (Captain Asai, flagship *Shirakumo*)
Destroyers *Shirakumo*, *Asashio* (both Shirakumo class), *Kasumi*, *Akatsuki** (both Akatsuki class)
2nd Destroyer Division (Commander Ishida)
Destroyers *Ikazuchi*, *Oboro*, *Inadzuma*, *Akebono* (all Ikazuchi class)
3rd Destroyer Division (Lieutenant-Commander Tsuchiya)
Destroyers *Usugumo*, *Shinonome* (both Murakumo class), *Sazanami* (Ikazuchi class)
1st Torpedo-boat Division (Lieutenant-Commander Seki)
Torpedo boats *Number 67*, *68*, *69**, *70* (all Number 67 class)
14th Torpedo-boat Division (Lieutenant-Commander Sakurai, flagship *Chidori*)
Torpedo boats *Chidori*, *Hayabusa*, *Manadzuru*, *Kasasagi* (all Hayabusa class)
Fleet Auxiliaries
1st Division
Gunboats *Oshima** (Oshima class), *Akagi* (Maya class)
Destroyer tender *Kasuga Maru*
Armed merchant cruisers *Taichu Maru*, *Tainan Maru*
Repair ship *Miike Maru*
Hospital ship *Kobe Maru*
Cargo ships *Yamaguchi Maru*, *Fukuoka Maru*, *Kinshu Maru*, *Jinsen Maru*, *Bushio Maru*, *Buyo Maru*, *Tenshin Maru*, *Hokoku Maru*

Shikishima was one of the six Japanese battleships built in Britain prior to the Russo-Japanese War. Newer than the Fuji class, it was based on the British Majestic-class battleship. (USNHHC)

2nd Division
Destroyer tender *Nikko Maru*
Armed merchant cruisers *Hong Kong Maru*, *Nippon Maru*
Repair ship *Koto Maru*
Cargo ships *Taro Maru*, *Hikosan Maru*

SECOND FLEET

Vice Admiral Kamimura Hikonojo (flagship *Idzumo*)
2nd Division (Rear Admiral Misu Sotnio, flagship *Iwate*)
Armoured cruisers *Idzumo* (Idzumo class), *Adzuma* (Adzuma class), *Asama* (Asama class), *Yakumo* (Yakumo class), *Tokiwa* (Asama class), *Iwate* (Idzumo class)
Dispatch vessel *Chihaya* (Chihaya class)
4th Division (Rear Admiral Uryu Sotokichi, flagship *Naniwa*)
Protected cruisers *Naniwa* (Naniwa class), *Akashi* (Suma class), *Takachiho* (Naniwa class), *Niitaka* (Tsushima class)
4th Destroyer Division (Commander Nagai, flagship *Hayatori*)
Destroyers *Hayatori**, *Asagiri*, *Harusame*, *Murasame*, (all Harusame class)
5th Destroyer Division (Commander Mano, flagship *Murakumo*)
Destroyers *Murakumo*, *Shiranui*, *Yugiri*, *Kagero* (all Murakumo class)
9th Torpedo-boat Division (Commander Yashima, flagship *Aotaka*)
Torpedo boats *Aotaka*, *Hato*, *Kari*, *Tsubame* (all Aotaka class)
20th Torpedo-boat Division
Torpedo boats *Number 62*, *63*, *64*, *65* (all Number 39 class)

THIRD FLEET

Vice Admiral Kataoka Shichiro (flagship *Itsukushima*)
5th Division (Vice Admiral Kataoka Shichiro, flagship *Itsukushima*)
Battleship *Chinyen* (ex-Chinese Chen Yuan class)
Protected cruisers *Itsukushima* (Matsushima class), *Hashidate* (Matsushima class), *Matsushima* (Matsushima class)
6th Division (Rear Admiral Togo Masamichi, flagship *Izumi*)
Protected cruisers *Izumi* (ex-Chilean Esmeralda class), *Suma* (Suma class), *Akitsushima* (Akitsushima class), *Chiyoda* (Chiyoda class)
7th Division (Rear Admiral Hosoya, flagship *Fuso*)
Coastal defence ships *Fuso* (Fuso class), *Kaimon** (Kaimon class, screw corvette)
Protected cruiser *Saiyen** (ex-Chinese Chi Yuan class)
Miscellaneous gunboats
Gunboats *Heiyen** (ex-Chinese Ping Yuen class), *Tsukushi* (Tsukushi class), *Banjo* (Banjo class), *Chokai* (Maya class), *Atago** (Maya class), *Maya* (Maya class), *Uji* (Uji class), *Yaeyama* (Yaeyama class)
Dispatch vessel *Miyako* (Miyako class)
10th Torpedo-boat Division (Lieutenant-Commander Otaki, flagship *Number 43*)
Torpedo boats *Number 40*, *41*, *42*, *43* (all Number 39 class)
11th Torpedo-boat Division (Lieutenant-Commander Takebe, flagship *Number 73*)
Torpedo boats *Number 72*, *73*, *74**, *75** (all Number 67 class)
16th Torpedo-boat Division (Lieutenant-Commander Wakabayashi, flagship *Shirataka*)
Torpedo boats *Shirataka* (Shirataka class), *Number 71* (Number 67 class), *Number 39* and *66* (Number 39 class)
Attached ships
Destroyer tender *Toyohashi Maru*
Cargo ship *Ariake Maru*

In Transit

Armoured cruisers *Kasuga*, *Nisshin* (ex-Italian Mitra class)

Under construction

Protected cruisers *Otowa* (Otowa class), *Tsushima* (Tsushima class)

THE IMPERIAL RUSSIAN NAVY

RUSSIAN PACIFIC FLEET

1ST PACIFIC SQUADRON (PORT ARTHUR)

Vice Admiral Oskar Stark (flagship *Petropavlovsk*)
1st Sub-Division (Vice Admiral Oskar Stark)
Battleships *Petropavlovsk**, *Poltava**, *Sevastopol** (all Petropavlovsk class), *Tsesarevich* (Tsesarevich class)
2nd Sub-Division (Rear Admiral Prince Ukhtomsky, flagship *Petropavlovsk*)
Peresvyet*, *Pobeda** (both Peresvyet class), *Retvizan* (Retvizan class)
Division of Long-distance Scouts (Captain Viren, flagship *Bayan*)
Armoured cruisers *Bayan** (Bayan class) *Askold* (Askold class), *Diana*, *Pallada** (both Pallada class), *Varyag**[1] (Varyag class)
Division of Short-distance Scouts
Light cruiser *Boyarin** (Boyarin class)
Protected cruiser* *Novik* (Novik class)
Torpedo-gunboats *Vsadnik**, *Gaidamak** (both Kazarski class)
Minelayers *Amur**, *Yenisei** (Amur class)
1st Destroyer Flotilla
Destroyers *Bditelni*, *Bezposhtchadni*, *Bezshumni*, *Bezstrashni* (all Bezstrashni class), *Boevoi* (Boevoi class) *Boiki*, *Burni* (both Boiki class), *Grozovoi* (Vnimatelni class), *Leitenant Burakov* (Leitenant Burakov class), *Rastoropni*, *Razyashchi* (both Puilki class)

FLOATING DEFENCE OF PORT ARTHUR

2nd Destroyer Flotilla
Destroyers *Ryeshitelni*, *Serditi*, *Silni*, *Skori*, *Smyeli*, *Statni**, *Steregushchi*, *Storozhevoi*, *Strashni*, *Stroini* (all Puilki class), *Vlastni*, *Vnimatelni*, *Vnushitelni*, *Vuinoslivi* (all Vnimatelni class)

1 Detached on special service to Chemulpo.

Completed in 1898, *Petropavlovsk* was typical of Russian battleships of the late 19th century. *Petropavlovsk* was named in honour of one of the few Crimean War Russian naval victories, the Battle of Petropavlovsk-Kamchatka. It served as flagship for the 1st Pacific Squadron. (AC)

Gunboats and sloops

Gunboats *Gremyashchi*, *Otvajni* (both Grozyashchi class) *Gilyak*[2] (similar to Kubanetz class), *Djigit*, *Razboinik* (both Kreiser class), *Bobr* (Sivuch class)
Armed Merchant Cruiser *Zabiaka*
Auxiliary vessels
Hospital ship *Angara*
Transport *Mongolia*
Cargo ships *Silach*, *Kazan*

VLADIVOSTOK INDEPENDENT CRUISER SQUADRON

Rear Admiral Baron Shtakelberg (flagship *Rossiya*)
Armoured cruisers *Rossiya* (Rossiya class), *Rurik** (Rurik class), *Gromoboi* (Gromoboi class), *Bogatyr* (Bogatyr class)

FLOATING DEFENCE OF VLADIVOSTOK

Gunboats
Gunboats *Korietz**[3], *Mandjur**[4] (both Korietz class) *Sivuch*[5] (Sivuch class)
1st Torpedo-boat Division
Torpedo boats *Number 201*, *202* (Sutchena class), *203*, *204* (Sungari class), *205*, *206* (Sveaborg class)
2nd Torpedo-boat Division
Torpedo boats *Number 208*, *209*, *210*, *211* (Number 208–211 class)
Auxiliary Vessels
Armed merchant cruiser *Lena*
Transports *Manchuria*, *Argun*, *Shilka*, *Nonni*, *Kamchadal*, *Yakut*, *Tunguz*

NIKOLAIEVSK

Torpedo-boat Flotilla
Torpedo boats *Number 91*, *92*, *93*, *94*, *95*, *97*, *98* (1877–78 class)

In Transit[6]

Battleship *Oslyabya* (Peresvyet class)
Armoured cruisers *Dmitri Donskoi* (Dmitri Donskoi class), *Aurora* (Pallada class)
Destroyers *Bravi*, *Blestyashchi*, *Bodri*, *Buini*, *Bezuprechni*, *Byedovi* (all Boiki class)
Torpedo boats *Number 212*, *213* (212–213 class), *Number 221*, *222* (214–223 class)

2ND PACIFIC SQUADRON

Vice Admiral Zinovy Rozhestvensky (flagship *Kniaz Suvorov*)
1st Division (Vice Admiral Zinovy Rozhestvensky, flagship *Kniaz Suvorov*)
Battleships *Kniaz Suvorov**, *Imperator Alexandr III**, *Borodino**, *Oryel** (all Borodino class)
2nd Division (Rear Admiral Baron Dimitry von Folkersam, flagship *Oslyabya*)
Battleships *Oslyabya** (Peresvyet class), *Sisoi Veliky** (Sisoi Veliky class), *Navarin** (Navarin class)
Armoured cruiser *Admiral Nakhimov** (Admiral Nakhimov class)
1st Cruiser Division (Rear Admiral Oskar Enkvist, flagship *Oleg*)
Armoured cruisers *Oleg* (Bogatyr class), *Aurora* (Pallada class), *Dmitri Donskoi** (Dmitri Donskoi class)
Attached Cruisers
Protected cruisers *Izumrud**, *Zhemchug* (Izumrud class), *Svyetlana** (Svyetlana class)
Destroyer Flotilla
1st Destroyer Division
Destroyers *Byedovi**, *Buini**, *Bravi*, *Buistri** (all Boiki class)

2 Built in 1896 as a large river gunboat.
3 Detached on special service to Chemulpo.
4 Detached on special service to Shanghai.
5 Detached on special service to Newchwang.
6 All returned to St Petersburg once war was declared.

2nd Destroyer Division
Destroyers *Blestyashchi**, *Bezuprechni**, *Bodri*, *Gromki*, *Grozni**
(Boiki class)
Transport Squadron (Captain Radlov, flagship *Almaz*)
Protected yacht *Almaz* (Almaz class)
Transports *Anaduir*, *Irtuish**
Repair ship *Kamchatka**
Ammunition ship *Koreya*
Tugs *Rus**, *Svir*
Hospital ships *Orel*, *Kostroma*

3RD PACIFIC SQUADRON
Rear Admiral Nikolai Ivanovich Nebogatov (flagship *Imperator Nikolai I*)
1st Division[7] (Rear Admiral Nikolai Ivanovich Nebogatov, flagship *Imperator Nikolai I*)
Battleships *Imperator Nikolai I** (Imperator Aleksandr II class), *General Admiral Apraksin**, *Admiral Senyavin**, *Admiral Ushakov** (all Admiral Ushakov class)
Attached cruisers
Armoured cruiser *Vladimir Monomakh** (Vladimir Monomakh class)
Armed merchant cruiser *Ural** (formerly the *Kaiserin Maria Theresia*)

SPECIFIC BATTLES

BATTLE OF THE YELLOW SEA (10 AUGUST 1904)
Japanese Combined Fleet (Vice Admiral Togo Heihachiro, flagship *Mikasa*)
1st Division (Rear Admiral Nashiha Tokioki, flagship *Hatsuse*)
Battleships *Mikasa*, *Asahi*, *Fuji*, *Shikishima*
Armoured cruisers *Kasuga*, *Nisshin*
Dispatch vessel *Yaeyama*
3rd Division (Rear Admiral Dewa Shigeto, flagship *Yakumo*)
Armoured cruiser *Yakumo*
Protected cruisers *Chitose*, *Takasago*, *Kasagi*
5th Division (Vice Admiral Kataoka Shichiro, flagship *Hashidate*)
Battleship *Chinyen*
Protected cruisers *Hashidate*, *Matsushima*, *Asama*
6th Division (Rear Admiral Togo Masamichi, flagship *Akashi*)
Protected cruisers *Akashi*, *Suma*, *Akitsushima*, *Izumi*
1st Destroyer Division (Captain Asai, flagship *Asashio*)
Destroyers *Shirakumo*, *Asashio*, *Kasumi*
2nd Destroyer Division (Commander Ishida, flagship *Ikazuchi*)
Destroyers *Ikazuchi*, *Oboro*, *Inadzuma*, *Akebono*
3rd Destroyer Division (Lieutenant-Commander Tsuchiya)
Destroyers *Usugumo*, *Shinonome*, *Sazanami*
4th Destroyer Division (Commander Nagai, flagship *Hayatori*)
Destroyers *Hayatori*, *Asagiri*, *Harusame*, *Murasame*
5th Destroyer Division (Commander Mano, flagship *Kagero*)
Destroyers *Murakumo*, *Shiranui*, *Yugiri*, *Kagero*
1st Torpedo-boat Division (Lieutenant-Commander Seki, flagship *Number 69*)
Torpedo boats *Number 67, 68, 69, 70*
2nd Torpedo-boat Division
Torpedo boats *Number 37, 38, 46, 45*
6th Torpedo-boat Division
Torpedo boats *Number 56, 57, 58, 59*
10th Torpedo-boat Division (Lieutenant-Commander Otaki, flagship *Number 43*)
Torpedo boats *Number 40, 41, 42, 43*
14th Torpedo-boat Division (Lieutenant-Commander Sakurai, flagship *Chidori*)
Torpedo boats *Chidori*, *Hayabusa*, *Manadzuru*, *Kasasagi*
16th Torpedo-boat Division (Lieutenant-Commander Wakabayashi, flagship *Shirataka*)
Torpedo boats *Shirataka*, *Number 39, 66, 71*

20th Torpedo-boat Division (Commander Arakawa, flagship *Number 62*)
Torpedo boats *Number 62, 63, 64, 65*
21st Torpedo-boat Division
Torpedo boats *Number 44, 47, 49*
Russian 1st Pacific Squadron (Vice Admiral Wilgelm Vitgeft, flagship *Tsesarevich*)
1st Sub-Division (Vice Admiral Wilgelm Vitgeft)
Battleships *Tsesarevich*, *Retvizan*, *Pobeda*
2nd Sub-Division (Rear Admiral Prince Ukhtomsky, flagship *Peresvyet*)
Battleships *Peresvyet*, *Poltava*, *Sevastopol*
Division of Long-distance Scouts (Captain Viren, flagship *Askold*)
Armoured cruisers *Askold*, *Diana*, *Pallada*
Division of Short-distance Scouts
Protected cruiser *Novik*
Destroyer Flotilla
Protected cruiser *Novik*
Destroyers *Bezposhtchadni*, *Bezshumni*, *Bezstrashni*, *Boiki*, *Burni*, *Grozovoi*, *Vlastni*, *Vuinoslivi*

BATTLE OF TSUSHIMA (27–28 MAY 1905)
Japanese Combined Fleet (Vice Admiral Togo Heihachiro, flagship *Mikasa*)
1st Division (Vice Admiral Togo Heihachiro, flagship *Mikasa*)
Battleships *Mikasa*, *Asahi*, *Fuji*, *Shikishima*
Armoured cruisers *Kasuga*, *Nisshin*
Dispatch vessel *Tatsuta*
2nd Division (Vice Admiral Kamimura Hikonojo, flagship *Idzumo*)
Armoured cruisers *Idzumo*, *Adzuma*, *Tokiwa*, *Yakumo*, *Asama*, *Iwate*
Dispatch vessel *Chihaya*
3rd Division (Rear Admiral Dewa Shigeto, flagship *Chitose*)
Protected cruisers *Chitose*, *Kasagi*, *Niitaka*, *Otowa*
4th Division (Rear Admiral Uryu Sotokichi, flagship *Naniwa*)
Protected cruisers *Naniwa*, *Akashi*, *Takachiho*, *Tsushima*
5th Division (Vice Admiral Kataoka Shichiro, flagship *Itsukushima*)
Battleship *Chinyen*
Protected cruisers *Itsukushima*, *Hashidate*, *Matsushima*
Dispatch vessel *Yaeyama*
6th Division (Rear Admiral Togo Masamichi, flagship *Izumi*)
Protected cruisers *Izumi*, *Suma*, *Akitsushima*, *Chiyoda*
1st Destroyer Division (Commander Nagai, flagship *Hayatori*)
Destroyers *Harusame*, *Fubuki*, *Ariake*, *Akatsuki*

The armoured cruiser *Gromoboi* was designed as a long-range commerce raider. Commissioned in 1900, it was sent to the Pacific almost immediately afterwards, serving in the Vladivostok Independent Cruiser Squadron. It served as a minelaying cruiser in the Baltic during World War I. (AC)

---

7   Renamed 3rd Division after fleet merger.

2nd Destroyer Division (Commander Ishida, flagship *Ikazuchi*)
Destroyers *Ikazuchi, Oboro, Inadzuma, Akebono*
3rd Destroyer Division (Lieutenant-Commander Tsuchiya)
Destroyers *Usugumo, Shinonome, Sazanami, Kasumi*
4th Destroyer Division (Commander Nagai, flagship *Hayatori*)
Destroyers *Asagiri, Murasame, Shirakumo, Asashio*
5th Destroyer Division (Commander Mano, flagship *Kagero*)
Destroyers *Murakumo, Shiranui, Yugiri, Kagero*
1st Torpedo-boat Division (Lieutenant-Commander Seki, flagship *Number 69*)
Torpedo boats *Number 67, 68, 69, 70*
2nd Torpedo-boat Division
Torpedo boats *Number 38, 37, 46, 45*
6th Torpedo-boat Division
Torpedo boats *Number 56, 57, 58, 59*
9th Torpedo-boat Division (Commander Yashima, flagship *Aotaka*)
Torpedo boats *Aotaka, Hato, Kari, Tsubame*
10th Torpedo-boat Division (Lieutenant-Commander Otaki, flagship *Number 43*)
Torpedo boats *Number 40, 41, 42, 43*
11th Torpedo-boat Division (Lieutenant-Commander Takebe, flagship *Number 73*)
Torpedo boats *Number 72, 73, 74, 75*
15th Torpedo-boat Division
Torpedo boats *Hibari, Sagi, Hashitaki, Uzura*
Russian Pacific Fleet (Vice Admiral Zinovy Rozhestvensky, flagship *Kniaz Suvorov*)
1st Division (Vice Admiral Zinovy Rozhestvensky, flagship *Kniaz Suvorov*)
Battleships *Kniaz Suvorov, Imperator Alexandr III, Borodino, Oryel*
2nd Division (Rear Admiral Baron Dimitri von Folkersam, flagship *Oslyabya*)
Battleships *Oslyabya, Sisoi Veliky, Navarin*
Armoured cruiser *Admiral Nakhimov*

3rd Division (Rear Admiral Nikolai Ivanovich Nebogatov, flagship *Imperator Nikolai I*)
Battleships *Imperator Nikolai I, General Admiral Apraksin, Admiral Senyavin, Admiral Ushakov*
1st Cruiser Division (Rear Admiral Oskar Enkvist, flagship *Oleg*)
Armoured cruisers *Oleg, Aurora, Dmitri Donskoi*
Attached cruisers
Armoured cruiser *Vladimir Monomakh*
Protected cruisers *Izumrud, Zhemchug, Svyetlana*
Armed merchant cruiser *Ural*
Destroyer Flotilla:
1st Destroyer Division
Destroyers *Byedovi, Buini, Bravi, Buistri*
2nd Destroyer Division
Blestyashchi, Bezuprechni, Bodri, Gromki, Grozni
Transport Squadron (Captain Radlov, flagship *Almaz*)
Protected yacht *Almaz*
Transports *Anaduir, Irtuish*
Repair ship *Kamchatka*
Ammunition ship *Koreya*
Tugs *Rus, Svir*
Hospital ships *Orel, Kostroma*

Niitaka was typical of the protected cruisers Japan built domestically between 1898 and 1905. Completed just before the Russo-Japanese War started, *Niitaka* saw action at Chemulpo Bay, the Battle of Ulsan, and the Battle of Tsushima. (USNHHC)

OPPOSING PLANS

The naval war plans of both Japan and Russia were influenced by a book on naval strategy that appeared in 1890: Alfred Thayer Mahan's *The Influence of Sea Power in History, 1660–1783*. It was the first major conflict involving sea power that occurred after the book's publication. The book stressed the need for a navy to secure command of the sea. It stated that the latter could be achieved through both the destruction of a nation's maritime commerce, but also by destroying the enemy fleet.

Each nation's navy drew a different lesson from the book. Japan pursued the goal of neutralizing or destroying the Imperial Russian Navy, preferably through a single decisive battle. Russia fixated on maintaining a fleet in being, and believed the mere existence of its fleet put Japan's command of the sea at risk. The plans of both nations were filtered through these strategies.

Japan and Russia had fundamental differences about fighting naval wars. Japan always sought a single decisive battle, whereas Russia sought to preserve its battle line until it could attack with overwhelming strength. One result was that the two fleets' minor warships fought most of the initial actions. (AC)

JAPANESE

Japan's plans at Tsushima were dictated by its military goals: controlling the Korean Peninsula and capturing the Liaodong Peninsula. The former was Japan's primary war goal. The latter was seen as the best way to ensure control of Korea, as it deprived Russia of Port Arthur, its principal Pacific naval base, restoring the port to Japan.

Throughout the war, Japan had to project power and place large armies, supplied from Japan, on the Asian mainland. The Imperial Japanese Navy's initial role was to land the army on Asian shores and then supply it. Once this was accomplished, the navy had to keep ocean communications with Japan open. All this required Japan to control the Sea of Japan, the Yellow Sea and the Pacific waters off the coast of Japan.

This required neutralizing the Imperial Russian Navy in those areas. The task was made more difficult because the Russian Navy in Pacific waters outnumbered the Japanese Navy with (on paper) more powerful warships. At the outset of the Russo-Japanese War, the Russian 1st Pacific Squadron at Port Arthur alone outnumbered the Japanese Combined Fleet. Russia also had a cruiser squadron at Vladivostok. Had the 2nd Pacific Squadron been dispatched sooner and rendezvoused with the 1st Pacific Squadron before Port Arthur fell, Japan could not have controlled the Yellow Sea.

The overarching strategic goal of the Imperial Japanese Navy was to control the waters around Korea and Manchuria so the Imperial Japanese Army could land and maintain an army on the Asian mainland. (AC)

The overall war plan for the Imperial Japanese Navy focused on neutralizing Russian advantages. The two broad principles followed by Japan were to seek opportunities to destroy parts of the Russian Navy in detail and keep the rest of it, particularly the 1st Pacific Squadron, in harbour.

This strategy was executed in the war's opening stages by launching a night-time torpedo attack against the 1st Pacific Squadron at its anchorage outside Port Arthur. Had it been successful, it would have reversed the naval balance of power in one stroke. Japan attacked the ships of the 1st Pacific Squadron that Russia routinely stationed in Chinese and Korean ports. While these ships were not major units – they were gunboats and a cruiser – Japan went after them in the opening days of the war to prevent them from going to sea, if they could not be destroyed.

Most notably, Japan sent a division of cruisers after the Russian ships stationed at Chemulpo (modern Inchon), the armoured cruiser *Varyag* and the gunboat *Korietz*. Japan also forced the internment of the gunboat at Shanghai and caused the gunboat at Newchuang to flee up the Liao River and exit the war. A minor three-day effort cost Russia four warships.

Japan followed a similar strategy to mask the Vladivostok Squadron, an independent Russian force of four armoured cruisers. Six armoured cruisers and four protected cruisers covered these ships. The Vladivostok cruisers were forced to steam together rather than individually. Had the Vladivostok Squadron been able to make individual cruises, Japanese transport and cargo losses would have been unacceptably high. The Japanese cruisers were also stationed at Tsushima, covering the sea routes that Japanese troop transports and supply ships were taking. It was not universally successful, but it was an economical use of the force available to Japan.

Maintaining a close blockade of Port Arthur required an anchorage within a few hours' steaming of Port Arthur. Togo seized the Elliot Islands, small landforms off the Liaodong Peninsula. The location of the anchorage was kept secret during the war, with the cooperation of friendly war correspondents. (AC)

Japan focused most of its efforts on containing the Russian battle fleet. It allocated all its battleships, its two most modern armoured cruisers, its remaining modern protected cruisers and most of its torpedo craft to the Yellow Sea and to the blockade of Port Arthur. To allow its fleet to remain continuously off Port Arthur, Togo seized the Elliot Islands off the Liaodong Peninsula as an anchorage and coaling station. These islands were only a few hours steaming from Port Arthur. Without this advanced base, Japan could not have maintained its close blockade. (The base was later moved to Dalny – modern Dalian – further up the Liaodong Peninsula once that harbour had been captured by the Japanese Army.)

The blockade was mounted by order of the Japanese imperial staff. Togo wanted to lure the Russians out of Port Arthur and fight a decisive battle to sink its fleet. The imperial staff considered it to be too risky, preferring to keep the 1st Pacific Squadron penned in Port Arthur's inner harbour. Several unsuccessful efforts to place blockships in the channel exiting Port Arthur were made. These would have trapped the Russians inside the harbour.

Japan achieved all of its naval objectives before the 2nd Pacific Squadron entered the Indian Ocean. The 1st Pacific Squadron had been eliminated with the capture of Port Arthur. The Vladivostok Squadron had been de-fanged. One cruiser had been sunk, two damaged too badly to be combat worthy and the remaining cruiser too weak to sortie alone. The approach of the new Russian fleet offered new challenges.

There was the problem of intercepting it, although a straightforward solution was soon devised. Once in Asian waters, it had only one destination:

Port Arthur was Russia's long-sought ice-free port in the Pacific. This is a picture of its inner basin in 1904. Its workshops, storehouses, and dry dock made it the Imperial Russian Navy's most important Pacific bastion. (USNHHC)

Vladivostok. There were several ways to reach Vladivostok from Indochina, but only one practical route: through the Tsushima Strait.

More challenging was actually fighting the Russian fleet. In January 1905, Japan's warships had been worn out by a year's fighting and hard sea service. Fortunately the Russians arrived at Indochina in late April, and Japan managed to refit its entire fleet during that period. By the beginning of May, it was ready, restored to fighting condition.

Togo based his fleet at Pusan in Korea, while setting a picket line of cruisers and scouts at the southern approaches of the Tsushima Strait. This allowed the Russian fleet to be spotted and its course plotted in time to allow the Japanese fleet to intercept.

RUSSIAN

Russia had everything needed to win the naval part of the Russo-Japanese War. It had more ships, a professional officer corps, trained crews, adequate stores of supplies and ammunition, and secure bases from which to operate. It lacked only one thing: a plan. As a result, it lost.

Imperial Russia did not expect a war with Japan. This was partly due to an appreciation of Russian naval and military strength in the Far East, and partly a fatal underestimation of Japanese capabilities and determination. Russia lacked a plan to deal with the Imperial Japanese Navy (other than intimidate it into non-belligerency) because it did not believe it needed one. When Japan did attack, the initial Russian reaction was shock followed by inaction.

The majority of Russia's senior naval officers viewed the navy as an asset to be preserved, keeping it as a fleet in being. It would be committed to battle only when everything was ready and only against a badly outnumbered enemy. This meant it would almost never be used, as conditions were never quite right to commit the fleet.

According to the admirals in charge, the Russian strategy pursued was to let the Japanese Navy exhaust itself blockading Port Arthur. The hazards of the sea, aided by Russian mines, would reduce the Japanese Navy to an acceptable size, at which point it could be attacked with overwhelming force. This was a defendable plan, especially during the opening stages of the war, before Port Arthur was isolated and put under siege. Russia was a world leader in naval mines. The Yellow Sea was also hazardous during the winter and early spring months.

However, Japan's Elliot Islands advanced base undercut part of the basis for the strategy. Japanese ships did not need to sail 500 nautical miles to Port Arthur from Japan, but only about 50 from the Elliot Islands. This strategy also ceded control of the seas to Japan. It allowed Japan to land an army on the Asian mainland. The Russian Army proved incapable of stopping the Japanese.

Once Port Arthur was cut off, especially after it was put under close siege, simply maintaining the 1st Pacific Squadron as a fleet in being, skulking in the inner harbour, became unviable. A fleet in being requires a safe harbour. At that point, the battle fleet should have left Port Arthur either to challenge the blockading fleet or to depart for Vladivostok, which was not under siege. Remaining passively in port guaranteed the loss of the ships once the port fell.

Others, most notably Vice Admiral Stepan Makarov but also including Vice Admiral Zinovy Rozhestvensky, believed in a more aggressive use of the Russian fleet. Makarov in particular used the fleet aggressively against Japan. He believed the 1st Pacific Squadron was strong enough to defeat Togo's forces. Makarov had the fleet sortie almost daily and kept them constantly on the move. He felt this would improve crew quality and morale. Successful sea operations provided the crews with experience and confidence.

Unfortunately, Makarov did not arrive until after Japan had landed its army. Use of the 1st Pacific Squadron in the aggressive manner sought by Makarov during the first weeks of the war might have delayed or even deterred the Japanese landings in Manchuria. Even more unfortunately, Makarov was killed in battle within a month of his arrival. Thereafter the 1st Pacific Squadron reverted to its passive fleet-in-being strategy, except for one sortie, ordered by the Kremlin, in August 1904.

The dispatch of the 2nd Pacific Squadron was more evidence of a lack of a Russian plan. Preparations for sending reinforcements should have started immediately after the Japanese attack on Port Arthur. These would have included manning the ship to wartime complements, overhauling machinery and collecting ammunition and supplies. The cost, even if the decision was made not to send the ships, would have been trivial. Due to the distances involved, any reinforcement had to start early or risk arriving after it was too late to make a difference.

Vice Admiral Wilgelm Vitgeft was an advocate of maintaining a fleet-in-being. Upon assuming naval command after Makarov's death, Vitgeft withdrew Russian major units from the Port Arthur roadstead, keeping them in the inner harbour to protect them. (AC)

Instead, the decision to reinforce the 1st Pacific Squadron was not made until June and no preparations were completed before then. The 2nd Pacific Squadron did not leave until October. By then, Port Arthur had been completely invested. Had it left at the start of June and not been slowed down waiting for the 3rd Pacific Squadron, it could have arrived by October, when it might have made a difference.

The fall of Port Arthur occurred when the reinforcements were at Madagascar, halfway to their destination. The strategic reason for sending reinforcements disappeared with Port Arthur's loss, yet the fleet was not withdrawn. Instead, it was ordered to a still more distant destination, Vladivostok. Furthermore, it was ordered to wait for the 3rd Pacific Squadron, which gave the Japanese time to refit their war-worn fleet. By the time the Russians appeared in Asian waters, their ships were decrepit due to the long voyage with inadequate maintenance. While Rozhestvensky made the best tactical plans he could in the situation in which he was placed, the results of Tsushima were almost inevitable.

THE CAMPAIGN

The Battle of Tsushima cannot be understood in isolation. It can only be understood when examined within the context of the entire naval phase of the Russo-Japanese War. Tsushima was the most decisive surface naval action of the 20th century. Of 38 participating Russian ships, which included eight battleships and six other armoured warships, only three reached Vladivostok after the battle. Every Russian capital ship was sunk or captured. By contrast, Japanese losses were minimal, with three torpedo boats sunk.

What makes this more remarkable was Tsushima was virtually the only tactically decisive naval action fought during the Russo-Japanese War. Only one major surface warship had been lost during a surface battle up to Tsushima, by either side, although both sides lost destroyers. With the exception of *Rurik*, sunk at the Battle of Ulsan, every warship larger than a destroyer lost was scuttled in port to prevent capture, destroyed through shipwreck, or sunk by mines. At the Battle of the Yellow Sea, an action on the scale of Tsushima, not one ship was sunk by either side.

Additionally, while the Russian Pacific Fleet rarely came out as well as the Japanese in a tactical exchange, generally each battle was close, with both sides taking significant damage. At the end of the Battle of the Yellow Sea,

Although Russian and Japanese warships fought numerous times in 1904, not one major warship was sunk by gunfire or torpedoes. Losses were caused by mines, collisions or grounding. Sometimes, as at Chemulpo, ships were scuttled to prevent capture. (LOC)

both sides had been severely battered. At Tsushima, the Russian fleet was virtually ineffective.

OPENING DAYS, 8–9 FEBRUARY 1904

Shortly after midnight on 9 February 1904, four Japanese destroyers slid into the roadstead at Port Arthur. Anchored there were the main elements of the Russian 1st Pacific Squadron: seven battleships and six cruisers. The Russian warships had anchor watches set. Most of the crews were asleep; many of the officers were aboard the flagship, battleship *Petropavlovsk*, attending a birthday party that Vice Admiral Oskar Stark, commander of the Russian Pacific Fleet, was hosting for his wife.

Precautions taken by the Russian Pacific that night were routine. Three Russian destroyers were patrolling outside Port Arthur and the anti-torpedo nets carried by each warship were deployed. The cruiser *Askold*, moored furthest out in the roadstead, was the duty ship. Most of the destroyers and torpedo boats were snugly secured in Port Arthur harbour or in the channel linking the harbour with the roadstead.

These precautions seemed sufficient. Tensions were ratcheting up between Russia and Japan. War might break out in weeks, but the two nations were still at peace. When war started, Russia's ships would be guarded by the harbour's guns, even in the roadstead. These shore batteries were unmanned at night in peacetime, but would be continuously manned once war started. Anchored in the roadstead, the Russian fleet could steam against Japan's fleet once war began, without the delay entailed by leaving the harbour through a narrow, twisting channel.

However, Japan was already at war with Russia, although Russia did not yet realize this. The four Japanese destroyers were the first of ten sent to attack the Russian fleet in the roadstead. The attack was scheduled before any formal declaration of war, which would be delivered at St Petersburg three hours after the attack started.

Japan opened the war with a midnight attack on the Russian fleet anchored in Port Arthur's roadstead. Despite the advantage of surprise, only three hits were landed. (AC)

While controversial, attacking before declaring war did not violate international law in 1904. Declaring prior to the commencement of hostilities was not required until after the Second Hague Peace Conference in October 1907. Russia had used this loophole fewer than 100 years earlier, attacking Sweden before declaring war in 1809.

Once Japan decided Russia was negotiating in bad faith, it decided to go to war. Having made the decision, Japan sought a means to improve the odds of success in its favour. Crippling the Russian fleet at the war's outset would give Japan control of the seas. The original Japanese plan called for a surprise strike at Port Arthur with its battleships, cruisers and destroyers before declaring war, to catch the Russian fleet unaware.

A false report that Russia was expecting the attack led to an on-the-fly modification. Only the torpedo boats and destroyers would attack Port Arthur's anchorage during the night. In the morning, if reconnaissance indicated the Russian fleet was sufficiently crippled, Togo's battleships would mop up the survivors.

Ten of the 11 Japanese destroyers in the 1st, 2nd and 3rd Destroyer divisions were sent to Port Arthur after darkness fell on 8 February. Eight destroyers from the 4th and 5th Destroyer divisions went to Dalny, a Russian-controlled port further north on the Liaodong Peninsula, to guard against part of the Russian fleet having anchored there.

Things began going wrong almost immediately. An hour from Port Arthur, the Japanese destroyers stumbled over the patrolling Russian destroyers. Manoeuvring to avoid them, two Japanese destroyers collided and one became lost, reducing the strike force to eight. The Russian destroyers, under orders not to initiate hostilities, did not fire on the oddly located Japanese warships, and merely reported their presence (the reports were ignored by Port Arthur). The relieved Japanese disappeared into the night unmolested.

The Japanese broke into two groups as they neared Port Arthur. The first group hugged the shore and steamed up the eastern side of the moored Russian warships. Undetected, they fired into the Russian ships. Two torpedoes went straight and true. One struck the protected cruiser *Pallada* amidships. A second caught the battleship *Retvizan* in the bow. The other six missed, became entangled in torpedo nets or failed to explode.

The second set of destroyers fared worse. These destroyers skimmed the south side of the anchorage. Surprise had been lost after the first torpedo hit home. They only achieved one hit from eight torpedoes fired, which exploded on the bow of the battleship *Tsesarevich*. The destroyers came under increasing fire as the battle progressed.

The Russian fleet was in disarray, but not disabled. *Pallada*, *Retvizan* and *Tsesarevich* all needed repairs, but their guns still worked. By morning, when Rear Admiral Dewa reconnoitred Port Arthur with his cruisers, the Russians were ready to fight. Dewa noticed the confusion and three listing warships, and then signalled Togo that it was a good time to attack the Russians.

Togo brought his battleship into a hornet's nest. The *Boyarin*, on patrol, spotted the approaching Japanese warships, fired on *Mikasa* and fled, radioing warnings. As the Japanese came within gunnery range, their battleships opened up on Port Arthur's shore batteries with their main batteries, while the secondary guns and the cruisers concentrated on the Russian warships. The Russian ships all had steam up and came boiling out.

Togo realized his attack was premature. He landed some hits, but was receiving heavy fire. Reversing course, he drew out of range, with the Japanese battleships receiving several hits during this manoeuvre. The Russians took damage to four battleships and three cruisers. The battle ended indecisively.

One of the few decisive naval actions of 1904 was playing out in Korea as the Battle of Port Arthur was ending. Russia stationed two warships, the protected cruiser *Varyag* and the gunboat *Korietz*, at Chemulpo Bay (Inchon) in Korea. Then, as now, it was the port for Korea's capital Seoul. Several nations stationed warships there to protect the interests of their nationals: Britain, France, Japan and Italy kept a cruiser there. The United States stationed a gunboat and a collier there.

In addition to attacking the Russian fleet at Port Arthur, Japan opened the war by occupying Seoul, a first step in controlling the Korean Peninsula. Three transports carrying 2,500 troops steamed out of Japan, arriving off Chemulpo on 7 December. They were escorted by Rear Admiral Uryu

The protected cruiser *Varyag* and gunboat *Korietz* were stationed at Chemulpo when the war started. Driven back to Chemulpo by a superior Japanese task force, both ships were scuttled to prevent capture. *Varyag* opened its seacocks. (AC)

Sotokichi's 4th Cruiser Division reinforced by the armoured cruiser *Asama* and accompanied by eight torpedo boats. This fleet was joined by *Chiyoda*, the cruiser stationed at Chemulpo.

A Russian transport arriving at Chemulpo on 7 February reported the approaching ships. *Korietz* left port to investigate. Finding warships and assuming they were Russian, *Korietz* prepared to fire a salute. Realizing they were Japanese, *Korietz* retreated to port, but fired its guns. *Chiyoda* responded with a torpedo. Both sides missed.

The next day, the Japanese transports docked and began unloading troops at dusk. The two Russian warships allowed the troops to disembark, believing Russia and Japan were still at peace. Chemulpo was a neutral port, Korean not Russian, and thus Korea was the appropriate nation to refuse the landing, not Russia. As at Port Arthur, the commander of Russian naval forces at Chemulpo learned war had begun during the pre-dawn hours of 8 February. At 3.00am, the unloaded transports and Japanese warships steamed out of harbour. Only *Chiyoda* remained behind. It delivered an ultimatum to the senior Russian naval officer to leave Chemulpo before noon or face attack after 4.00pm. Copies of the ultimatum were sent to neutral warships present. The Japanese also urged the neutral warships to shift their anchorages away from *Varyag* and *Korietz*.

At noon, the captain of the British cruiser HMS *Talbot* visited Uryu's flagship, *Naniwa*, with a letter signed by almost all the neutral commanders in Chemulpo. It refused the request to shift anchorages on the grounds that Chemulpo was a neutral port. It hardly mattered. *Varyag*'s captain, Vsevolod Rudnev, resolved to attempt a fighting escape to Port Arthur. At 11.00am, an hour before the Japanese deadline, *Varyag* and *Korietz* raised steam and left port.

It was hopeless. *Korietz* could only make 10 knots. *Varyag* had 12 6in. and 12 3in. guns, while *Korietz* had two 8in. and one 6in. gun. They were facing an armoured cruiser and five protected cruisers, with two 8in. guns, 38 6in. guns and numerous smaller guns. The battle opened at 11.45am. Within 30 minutes *Varyag* received critical damage and by 12.45pm, the

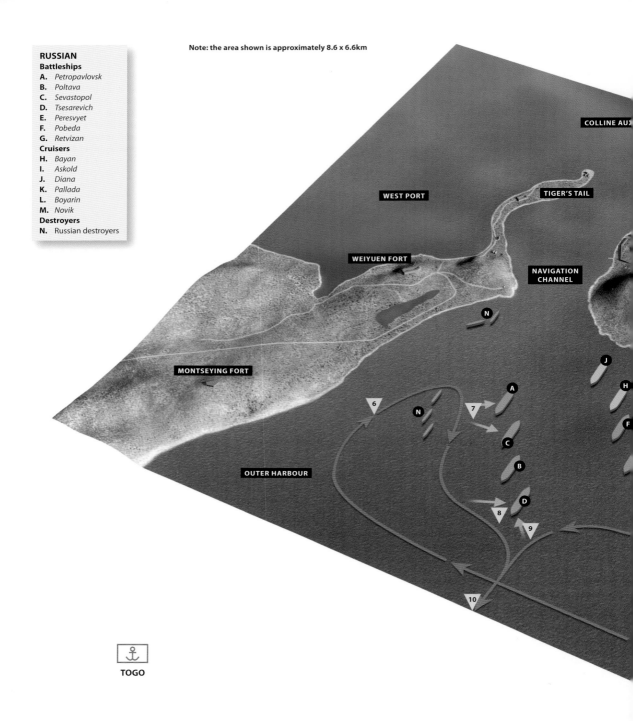

Note: the area shown is approximately 8.6 x 6.6km

RUSSIAN
Battleships
A. *Petropavlovsk*
B. *Poltava*
C. *Sevastopol*
D. *Tsesarevich*
E. *Peresvyet*
F. *Pobeda*
G. *Retvizan*
Cruisers
H. *Bayan*
I. *Askold*
J. *Diana*
K. *Pallada*
L. *Boyarin*
M. *Novik*
Destroyers
N. Russian destroyers

COLLINE AUX

TIGER'S TAIL

WEST PORT

WEIYUEN FORT

NAVIGATION CHANNEL

MONTSEYING FORT

OUTER HARBOUR

TOGO

▼ EVENTS

1. 12.23am: four Japanese destroyers of the 1st Destroyer Division enter the harbour.

2. *Askold*, serving as guard ship, challenges Japanese but receives no response.

3. Four destroyers of the 3rd Destroyer Division enter the harbour.

4. Four torpedoes are launched against *Pallada*. One hits amidships causing significant damage.

5. Four torpedoes are launched against *Retvizan*. One hits forward, causing minor damage.

6. 3rd Destroyer Division steams to shoal line, then doubles back.

7. Torpedoes are fired at *Petropavlovsk* and *Sevastopol*, but miss.

8. Torpedoes are fired at *Tsesarevich*, but miss.

9. Two further torpedoes are fired at *Tsesarevich*; this time, one hits near the bow.

10. Japanese destroyers exit the harbour.

SURPRISE ATTACK ON PORT ARTHUR, 8–9 FEBRUARY 1904

On the evening of 8–9 February, Japan attacked the Russian fleet anchored in the roadstead of Port Arthur before hostilities were declared. The attack did relatively little damage due to the primitive torpedoes of 1904, which were unreliable, difficult to aim and easily foiled by anti-torpedo nets. Regardless, the psychological effect of the attack was decisive. It rocked the Russian Navy back on the defensive and instilled a belief in Japanese capabilities, which left the Russians timid and indecisive.

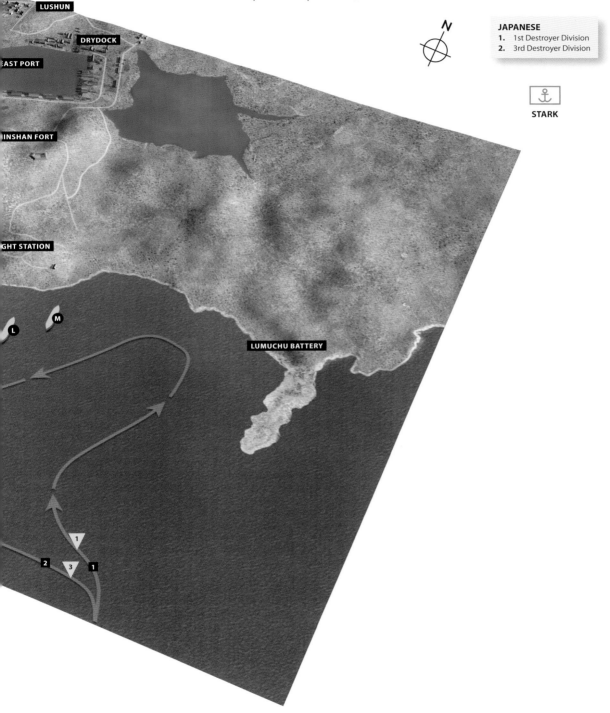

JAPANESE
1. 1st Destroyer Division
2. 3rd Destroyer Division

STARK

LUSHUN

DRYDOCK

EAST PORT

INSHAN FORT

GHT STATION

LUMUCHU BATTERY

battle was over; the two Russian warships were forced back to Chemulpo. All of *Varyag*'s guns were out of action. Nearly a quarter of its crew, 130 men, were casualties. *Korietz* was less badly damaged, but equally trapped. The Japanese fleet suffered almost no damage and no casualties.

At 4.00pm, *Korietz*'s crew scuttled the gunboat by exploding its powder rooms. The neutrals prevailed upon Rudnev not to blow up the *Varyag*, and it was scuttled by opening the seacocks, rolling over and sinking. Finally, the Russian transport that had arrived two days earlier was burned to prevent capture by the Japanese. Japan was now the master of Chemulpo and could reinforce its ground forces through the Yellow Sea without interference from the Imperial Russian Navy.

PORT ARTHUR BLOCKADED, FEBRUARY–AUGUST 1904

Japan's opening strikes failed to sink a single ship at Port Arthur. Despite that, the opening 24 hours of its war went well. Panicked Russian civilians were fleeing Port Arthur. Damage to the 1st Pacific Squadron was significant. Due to inadequate Russian repair facilities, the three torpedoed warships were out of the fight for several weeks. More importantly, the attacks intimidated the Russian fleet at Port Arthur into hiding in the inner harbour, destroyed the Russian naval forces in Korea and took two sister ships of *Korietz* out of the war. Japan was the master of Chemulpo and in control of the Yellow Sea.

While the 1st Pacific Squadron was down, it remained powerful enough to disrupt Japan's supply lines to the Asian mainland. This did not require fleet actions. Raiding cruisers and mines worked against transports. Russia had two cruisers built as minelayers, both stationed at Port Arthur. They were immediately sent out to protect Port Arthur and Dalny with minefields. An early effort ended tragi-comically. On 11 February, the minelaying cruiser *Yenisei* struck one of its own mines and sank. Attempting to assist *Yenisei*, the protected cruiser *Boyarin* struck another mine, was beached, abandoned, floated off, struck a second mine and sank.

It was a different story in the Sea of Japan. Russia had four cruisers stationed at Vladivostok. They conducted a total of six commerce-raiding sorties between February and August 1904. The first started the day after Japan attacked Port Arthur and swept the coast of Japan. Only one Japanese transport was found and sunk, but Japan's Second Fleet was unable to intercept the raiding Russians. A second sortie, which occurred between 24 February and 1 March, swept the Korean coast, but came back empty. Again, Japanese naval forces in the Sea of Japan missed the Russians.

The Combined Fleet returned to Sasebo after attacking Port Arthur. It briefly refuelled and

The Vladivostok Independent Cruiser Squadron swung into action almost immediately. It launched its first raid against Japanese cargo vessels the day hostilities commenced. It broke through the ice around the harbour to leave port. (AC)

Once the major Russian warships anchored within Port Arthur's harbour, the Japanese sought to trap them in by sinking blockships in the channel. The first attempt (shown) took place after dark on the night of 13/14 February. It was unsuccessful. (AC)

rearmed before returning. It was accompanied by five blockships, cargo ships loaded with stones and concrete, averaging 2,000 tons displacement. Port Arthur had only one narrow and shallow channel. Sinking the blockships in it would cork the 1st Pacific Squadron, now in the inner harbour, inside with no means of escape. The fleet arrived shortly before midnight on 23 February.

Early in the pre-dark hours of 24 February, the blockships steamed into the roadstead. As they approached the channel, they were detected, and gunfire from shore batteries and the *Retvizan* sank all five before they reached it. Two further attempts would be made to block the channel, one on 26 March and the second on 3 May. The ships were larger and faster on each successive try, but equally unsuccessful. Personnel losses increased with each attempt. In the first attempt, out of 70 sailors manning the blockships one was killed and three injured. On the third attempt, nearly half the 158 volunteers on the blockships were killed or captured.

The first failure to block the channel underscored the need for a convenient base where the Combined Fleet could watch Port Arthur. A close blockade was needed not just to prevent cruiser sorties or guard against a Russian fleet breakout, but also to prevent supplies from reaching Port Arthur. The nearest port outside the Home Islands controlled by Japan was the newly captured Chemulpo, 300 nautical miles and a day's steaming from Port Arthur.

To secure an anchorage closer to Port Arthur, Japan seized what were then known as the Elliot Islands, several small islands 15 miles off the Liaodong Peninsula, approximately 60 miles north-east of Port Arthur. Lightly populated and ungarrisoned by either China or Russia, they were perfectly situated to support a fleet blockading Port Arthur and Dalny. The location was kept secret.

Japan also attempted to close Vladivostok, bombarding it on 6 March. The bombardment, conducted by the 2nd Division reinforced by *Chinyen*, lasted 40 minutes but did little damage, missing the Russian cruisers entirely. More damage was done to the Vladivostok Independent Squadron a week later, when *Bogatyr* struck a rock in Amur Bay west of Vladivostok, damaging its bottom beyond the repair capabilities at Vladivostok. It sat

THE SINKING OF THE *PETROPAVLOVSK* (PP. 46–47)

If one event in the Russo-Japanese War could be said to have decisively affected its course, it would be the sinking of the battleship *Petropavlovsk*. This was less due to the loss of the battleship than due to the death of Vice Admiral Stepan Makarov, aboard *Petropavlovsk* when it was mined.

One of three of a class built between 1894 and 1899, *Petropavlovsk* (**1**) spent virtually its entire career with the Pacific Fleet, being sent to Port Arthur shortly after commissioning. It became the fleet's flagship when it arrived and served in that role throughout its existence. It was Vice Admiral Oskar Stark's flagship when Japanese torpedo boats attacked Port Arthur to open the war. The unfortunate Stark was hosting a birthday party for his wife aboard *Petropavlovsk* when the Japanese attack commenced.

Makarov replaced Stark. Before Makarov's arrival, the 1st Pacific Squadron responded ineptly to Japanese attacks. After his death, it behaved inertly. While Makarov was in command of the Pacific Fleet, it continuously and aggressively attacked the Japanese fleet. It is easy to imagine that this type of aggressive approach could have pushed the Imperial Japanese Navy to a breaking point, especially after the loss of *Hatsuse* and *Yashima* brought the number of Japanese battleships guarding Port Arthur down to three. After Makarov's death, the Russians returned to their previous, passive use of their navy, even abandoning the training programme Makarov instituted.

The loss of *Petropavlovsk* was due to a Japanese trap that partly miscarried. The Japanese laid mines across the entrance to Port

Arthur, intending the Russian fleet to hit them as they left port. Instead, the two battleships steaming out of Port Arthur missed the mines while leaving. It was only as they steamed back to Port Arthur that disaster struck. By then, *Petropavlovsk* and *Poltava* had been joined by three other battleships from Port Arthur, including *Pobeda*.

At 9.42am on 13 April, approaching the entrance to Port Arthur, *Petropavlovsk* steamed over the mine. It made contact next to the magazine. The exploding mine ripped a hole in *Petropavlovsk*'s bottom and then detonated the magazine. A column of smoke towered over *Petropavlovsk* from the subsequent explosion. Its bottom ripped open, and *Petropavlovsk* turned over and sank within minutes. Twenty-seven officers and 652 men went down with *Petropavlovsk*, including Makarov. Only 80 survivors – seven officers and 73 men – were pulled from the water.

Vasily Vereshchagin, a Russian war artist with an international reputation, was also aboard. At the admiral's invitation, Vereshchagin accompanied Makarov during the sortie to witness sea combat. He was among the dead.

The damage done by mines varied widely. Shortly after *Petropavlovsk* was ripped apart by its mine, *Pobeda* struck a mine while it was entering Port Arthur. Although flooding induced an 11-degree list, *Pobeda* was able to steam into harbour under its own power. It entered dry dock and its damage repaired by 9 June. Had Makarov been aboard *Pobeda* instead of *Petropavlovsk*, the war might have followed a very different course.

out the rest of the war, reducing the Vladivostok Independent Squadron's strength by one-quarter.

The need for closer Japanese monitoring at Port Arthur increased with the arrival of Stepan Makarov, one of the few Russian admirals to use his warships aggressively. Vice Admiral Stark had stood exclusively on the defensive since the opening day's battles, limiting his activities to minelaying, increasing the shore defences and a few destroyer sweeps. Russian morale plunged. Tsar Nicholas replaced Stark with Makarov on 24 February. Makarov arrived at Port Arthur on 8 March, taking command of the fleet the next day.

Makarov brought a new vitality to the Russian fleet. He began widespread training, improved readiness aboard the Russian warships and initiated frequent sorties from Port Arthur. The first was made on 9 March, when Makarov sent destroyers out to chase away Japanese destroyers. A short, sharp action took place, in which one Russian destroyer was lost, but this did not discourage the Russians, who were pleased to be striking back. Makarov moved the fleet back to the roadstead, where they could attack. Ships sortied virtually every day, aggressively patrolling the waters around Port Arthur. Morale soared over the next month. When the Japanese attempted to bombard Port Arthur by sea, Makarov sortied the fleet and chased them off.

The duels between Russian and Japanese became too predictable. The Russians sent out destroyers to fight Japan's inshore destroyers. Cruisers or battleships on both sides would reinforce. Then one side retired from the field if badly outnumbered. Over the next month, the Russians lost another destroyer, but seriously damaged *Fuji*. The Japanese knew where the Russian ships were likely to be. A few days before 13 April, they laid a minefield in the area.

That morning, when a patrolling Russian destroyer was attacked by the Japanese, Makarov led three battleships, four cruisers and a division of destroyers after the Japanese. The Russian force chased off the Japanese ships, which fell back to the Japanese battle line, the six battleships of Togo's 1st Division. Makarov broke off the battle. The Japanese, wary of taking damage, did not pursue. Returning to harbour, Makarov's flagship *Petropavlovsk* struck a mine, exploded and sank. Makarov was one of 679 men aboard who died. A second battleship, *Pobeda*, also struck a mine, but re-entered Port Arthur under its own power.

Japan instituted a close blockade on Port Arthur. They not only watched the Russian warships, but also intercepted any merchant traffic attempting to enter or leave. Here the *Asama* is shown capturing a Chinese junk running supplies into Port Arthur. (AC)

With Makarov's death, the 1st Pacific Squadron, now commanded by Vice Admiral Wilgelm Vitgeft, returned to passivity. Japan tightened its blockade of Port Arthur, stopping local coastal craft attempting to smuggle in goods. On 5 May, Japan landed troops at Pikou, a small fishing town on the Liaodong Peninsula that was 50 miles from Dalny and from the route of the Southern Manchuria Railway. The landing was massive and unopposed. The 1st Pacific Squadron swung at its moorings as 80 Japanese transports unloaded three divisions of troops with supporting artillery. Once established on their beachhead, Japanese troops began pushing towards Dalny and the railway.

Then fortune temporarily switched sides. The Vladivostok Independent Cruiser Squadron made another sweep down the Korean coast, catching several troop transports off Gensan (modern Wonsan). Although Japan only admitted the loss of the 600-ton *Goyo Maru*, the damage done was significant. In the Yellow Sea, the Russians were not the only navy falling into a pattern. As Japan tightened its blockade of Port Arthur, it brought its blockading warships closer. It finally established its picket line just past the range of Port Arthur's shore batteries. The captain of *Amur* noticed this. On 14 May, under cover of darkness, he sowed mines in the Japanese patrol area, his actions going unnoticed by the Japanese.

As the Japanese moved to their patrol positions that day, first *Hatsuse* and then *Yashima* struck the mines laid the previous night. *Hatsuse*'s magazines exploded after striking a second mine. The ship sank immediately, taking nearly 500 men with it. *Yashima* sank under tow to the Elliot Islands. The Imperial Japanese Navy lost one-third of its battleships in one day. *Fuji* was in the dockyard, being repaired, leaving just three battleships to guard the six remaining Russian battleships. Conversely, four previously damaged Russian battleships had completed repairs or had repairs nearing completion.

Japan concealed the loss of *Yashima* for over a year, pressing its two newest and most powerful armoured cruisers into the 1st Division to replace the lost battleships. This solution succeeded due to Russian naval inertia.

On 14 May 1904, the Japanese battleships *Hatsuse* (shown) and *Yashima* struck mines as they steamed to their patrol stations. *Hatsuse*'s magazines exploded and it sank within sight of the Russians at Port Arthur. (AC)

Russian naval inaction combined with Russian army incompetence allowed Japanese ground forces to advance down the Liaodong Peninsula and capture an unoccupied Dalny on 30 May. Warehouses and harbour facilities were abandoned intact, giving the Combined Fleet a sheltered, well-equipped port close to Port Arthur. Occupying Dalny also cut off Port Arthur from land communications with Russia, investing Port Arthur.

The only succor Port Arthur received was from the Vladivostok Independent Cruiser Squadron. On 15 June, during its third raid, it caught three Japanese transports in the Tsushima Straight. Two were sunk, including *Hitachi Maru* with over 1,000 troops and several 11in. siege howitzers intended for the siege of Port Arthur. A third transport, *Sado Maru* with 900 additional soldiers aboard, eventually grounded on Okinoshima. The next day, the squadron sank two sailing ships and captured the British steamship *Allanton*, carrying a cargo of coal. Despite several nearby Japanese cruisers, the Russians returned safely to Vladivostok, leaving the Japanese humiliated.

The Vladivostok Independent Cruiser Squadron mounted two more successful sorties in June and July, including one down the Pacific coast of Japan, passing through the Tsugaru Strait. These raids bagged three more transports. To stop the Russian cruisers, Japan assigned Vice Admiral Kamimura Hikonojo and the Second Fleet to run down the raiders.

By mid-June, repairs to all of the Russian battleships and cruisers damaged in the fighting between February and April had been completed. Keeping the 1st Pacific Squadron in Port Arthur was growing increasingly more dangerous. Under orders from St Petersburg, Admiral Vitgeft reluctantly had his fleet steam out of Port Arthur on 23 June. The Russian fleet in Port Arthur outgunned the Japanese fleet guarding them, with six battleships to the Japanese four. Yet when Togo closed to engage the emerging Russian fleet, Vitgeft decided he was outnumbered. Even if he was not, Vitgeft considered the Japanese torpedo boats too dangerous to fight. He ordered his ships back to Port Arthur, and there they remained until 10 August.

THE BATTLE OF THE YELLOW SEA, 10–14 AUGUST 1904

After the June attempt to sortie, Vitgeft decided his best course of action was to await reinforcement. The 1st Pacific Squadron swung at its moorings in Port Arthur's harbour, as conditions deteriorated. The Japanese Army pushed its siege lines closer to the harbour throughout July. Vitgeft waited passively, neglecting crew training and ignoring orders from his superior, Admiral Yevgeny Alexeiev, to move the ships to Vladivostok. Had Alexeiev been in Port Arthur, it would have been harder for Vitgeft to ignore him. Alexeiev had been called to St Petersburg for consultation shortly before the Japanese landings on the Liaodong Peninsula and was trapped outside Port Arthur by the Japanese advance.

On 7 August, an event occurred which forced Vitgeft to realize the fleet's peril: the Japanese brought their field guns close enough to bombard Port Arthur and shelled the harbour for the first time. Vitgeft was slightly wounded. Tsar Nicholas II, running out of patience, ordered Vitgeft to take the fleet to Vladivostok. On 10 August, Vitgeft reluctantly complied.

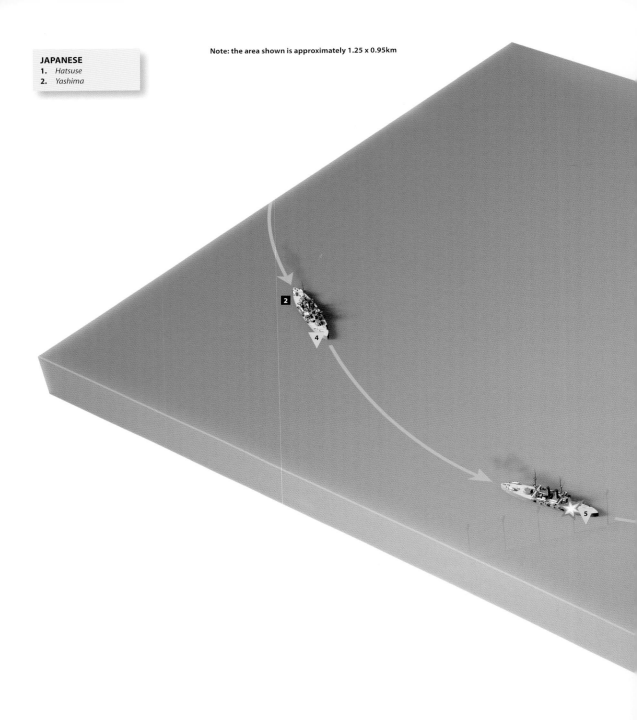

JAPANESE
1. *Hatsuse*
2. *Yashima*

Note: the area shown is approximately 1.25 x 0.95km

 EVENTS

1. During the night, Russian mine cruiser *Amur* lays a line of mines across the path Japanese warships take to bombard Port Arthur.

2. Leading a column of Japanese warships, at 10.50am *Hatsuse* hits a mine.

3. The mine disables its steering and stops the ship.

4. *Yashima* steams to the aid of *Hatsuse*.

5. *Yashima* strikes a mine that disables the aft starboard boiler room at approximately 11.00am.

6. *Yashima* strikes a second mine forward on the starboard side at 11.10am.

7. *Hatsuse* drifts into another mine at 12.30pm which detonates the magazine. *Hatsuse* sinks.

8. *Yashima* is towed to the Elliot Islands base, but sinks before reaching it.

SINKING OF THE *HATSUSE* AND *YASHIMA*

One month after *Petropavlovsk* was sunk by a mine, Japan suffered an even more severe reverse through mine warfare. Two of its six battleships struck mines sown the previous night, and sank. The opportunity arose due to Japanese arrogance and their underestimation of the creativity and audacity of their foe. Yet perhaps the Japanese were correct in their assessment of the Russians. Despite having struck a crippling blow to Togo's Combined Fleet, the Russians never took advantage of their opportunity. They remained passively in port, leaving only when ordered.

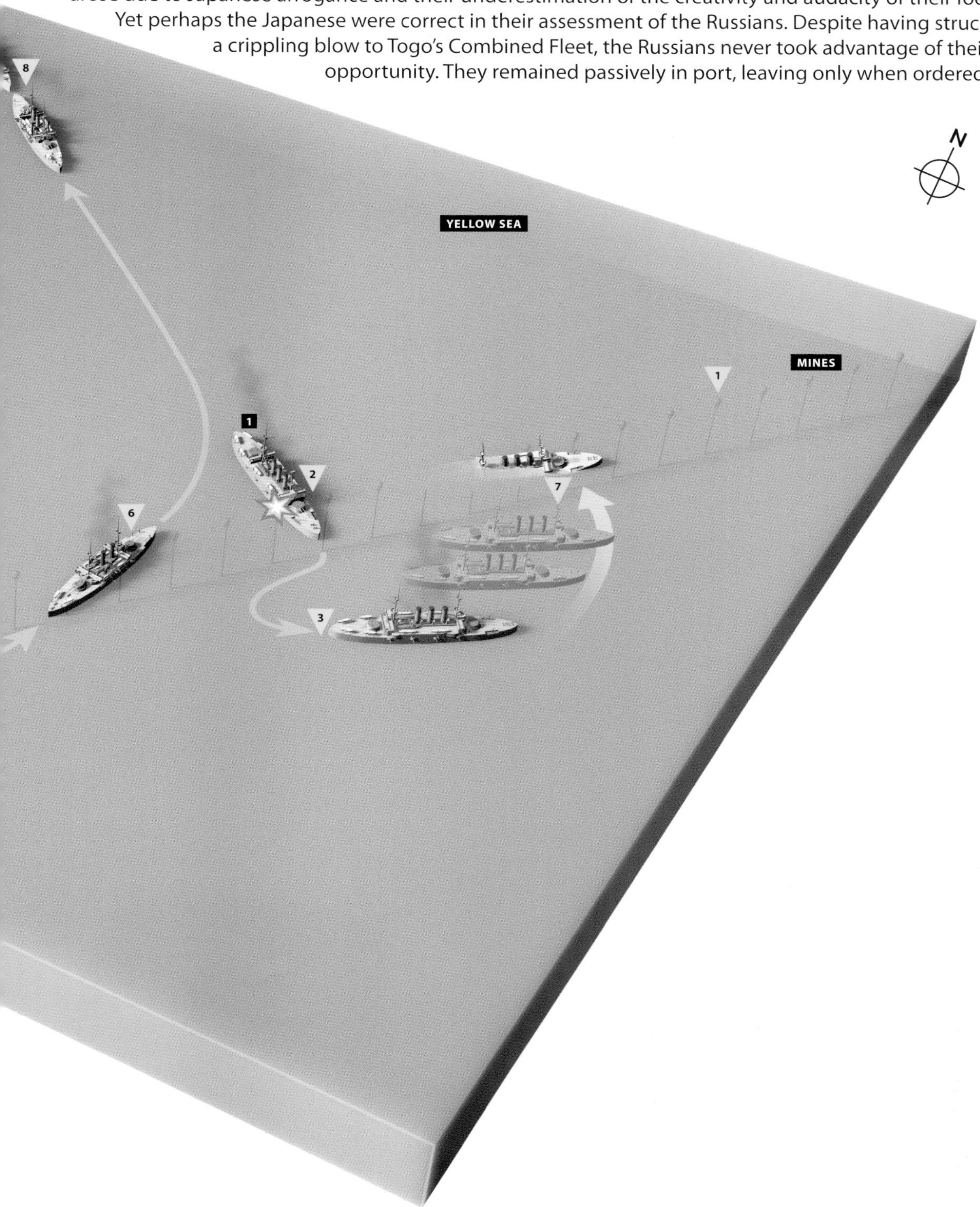

YELLOW SEA

MINES

N

Admiral Vitgeft repeatedly ignored orders to move the 1st Pacific Squadron to Vladivostok after May 1904. He finally obeyed on 10 August. The Russian fleet is shown leaving harbour on that day, its final departure from Port Arthur. (AC)

At the Battle of the Yellow Sea, both sides exchanged fire for nearly two hours. Despite the hundreds of 12in. shells fired, no ships were sunk by gunfire or even significantly slowed. (LOC)

At 6.15am Port Arthur time, Vitgeft's flagship *Tsesarevich* raised steam and began moving down the narrow channel at Port Arthur's entrance. It was followed by five other battleships and accompanied by four protected cruisers and 14 destroyers. Manoeuvring through the channel took time. It was nearly 10.00am before the fleet cleared the channel and was ready to

The Battle of the Yellow Sea.

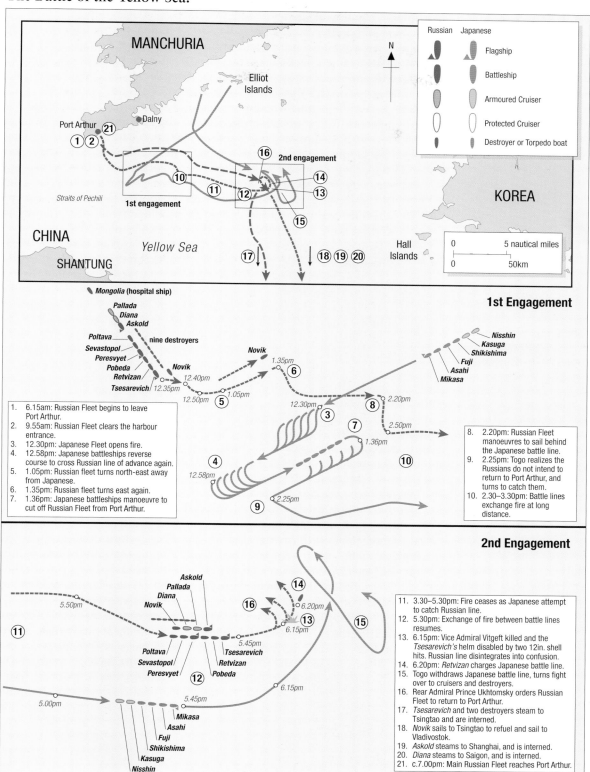

1st Engagement

1. 6.15am: Russian Fleet begins to leave Port Arthur.
2. 9.55am: Russian Fleet clears the harbour entrance.
3. 12.30pm: Japanese Fleet opens fire.
4. 12.58pm: Japanese battleships reverse course to cross Russian line of advance again.
5. 1.05pm: Russian fleet turns north-east away from Japanese.
6. 1.35pm: Russian fleet turns east again.
7. 1.36pm: Japanese battleships manoeuvre to cut off Russian Fleet from Port Arthur.

8. 2.20pm: Russian Fleet manoeuvres to sail behind the Japanese battle line.
9. 2.25pm: Togo realizes the Russians do not intend to return to Port Arthur, and turns to catch them.
10. 2.30–3.30pm: Battle lines exchange fire at long distance.

2nd Engagement

11. 3.30–5.30pm: Fire ceases as Japanese attempt to catch Russian line.
12. 5.30pm: Exchange of fire between battle lines resumes.
13. 6.15pm: Vice Admiral Vitgeft killed and the *Tsesarevich's* helm disabled by two 12in. shell hits. Russian line disintegrates into confusion.
14. 6.20pm: *Retvizan* charges Japanese battle line.
15. Togo withdraws Japanese battle line, turns fight over to cruisers and destroyers.
16. Rear Admiral Prince Ukhtomsky orders Russian Fleet to return to Port Arthur.
17. *Tsesarevich* and two destroyers steam to Tsingtao and are interned.
18. *Novik* sails to Tsingtao to refuel and sail to Vladivostok.
19. *Askold* steams to Shanghai, and is interned.
20. *Diana* steams to Saigon, and is interned.
21. c.7.00pm: Main Russian Fleet reaches Port Arthur.

proceed to sea. During that time, the smaller vessels swept the approaches for mines. The fleet set course south-west into the Yellow Sea.

It was impossible to miss the days of Russian preparation, and the Japanese were waiting for Vitgeft's ships. Togo chose not to oppose the Russian fleet as it left harbour for fear of scaring it back in. He saw Vitgeft's sortie as an opportunity for a single, decisive battle. He signalled his ships to assemble at Encounter Rock, a stone island at 38° 33' 60" N and 121° 37' E, named after the British warship which first mapped it.

Sailing south-east from Encounter Rock, Togo spotted Vitgeft's ships at 12.25pm, and five minutes later opened fire. Togo had the four surviving battleships of the 1st Division with the armoured cruisers *Kasuga* and *Nisshin* replacing the mined battleships. Dewa's protected cruiser of the 3rd Division as well as units of the Third Fleet added 11 protected cruisers, the elderly *Chinyen*, 18 destroyers and 30 torpedo boats to Togo's totals. Except for Dewa's four cruisers and the destroyers accompanying the 1st and 3rd divisions, these were unavailable when the battle started.

Togo swept south-east to cross the line of the Russian advance. Both fleets were in line of battle, with ships lined up behind the flagship. Under these circumstances, crossing the enemy's course (known as 'crossing the T') allowed the crossing ships to fire their entire broadside at the enemy, but only the bow guns of the enemy (and actually only the bow guns of the lead ship) could fire back, as the leading ships masked the trailing ones.

Vitgeft's initial course was intended to decoy Togo. Once Togo was committed to crossing the T, Vitgeft altered course to north-east. The two fleets were on parallel courses in opposite directions exchanging fire at extreme range. It looked as if Vitgeft might be able to slip past Togo's fleet after one exchange.

Togo then ordered a 180-degree turn to pursue the Russians. A line-ahead turn, expected by Vitgeft, where the flagship turned first and the rest of the line followed turning where the flagship did, would have put the Russians hopelessly ahead. Togo had his battle line turn together, putting the aft ship in the lead and the flagship at the rear. This kept the Russians in sight.

Vitgeft turned east at 1.36pm. When he noticed the pursuing Japanese, he recognized an opportunity to cross Togo's T and turned to steam across the oncoming Japanese line. Togo, realizing the danger, did a second 180-degree turn together and with his flagship *Mikasa* once more in the lead, turned east paralleling Vitgeft's course. Finally, at 2.30pm, Togo's line drew within range of Vitgeft's. For the next hour, the two fleets blazed away at 10,000 yards. Neither side did critical damage, but both sides landed solid hits, wearing each other down.

The wind was blowing from the north, with the smoke from the Russian line obscuring them, while the smoke from the Japanese ships blew away from the Russians. Togo, wanting to prevent the Russians from returning to Port Arthur, kept to the west of them, cutting off retreat. At 3.30pm, conditions became too bad for either side to spot the other. The two fleets drifted apart and fire ceased. The Russian line was slower than the Japanese. *Tsesarevich* and *Pobeda* had engine problems, slowing the entire fleet. But they continued east.

Togo finally realized the Russians were heading for Vladivostok, not Port Arthur. He sped past the slower Russian line. Having moved ahead, Togo closed to firing range. The two fleets resumed fire at 5.30pm and continued

firing for over an hour. No critical damage was done, but the accumulated damage was adding up. The Russian battleships *Poltava*, *Pobeda* and *Peresvyet* had taken heavy damage, but so had the Japanese *Mikasa* and *Asahi*. In the end, the battle had been going on so long that the Japanese shells, loaded with Shimose gunpowder, began detonating while in the overheated barrels of the battleship main guns.

Hoping to sink one Russian battleship, Togo ordered fire concentrated on *Pobeda*. This allowed the lead Russian battleships to concentrate on *Mikasa*. Togo ordered *Asahi* to take command of the fleet. Both sides were becoming incapable of fighting, but the Russians were still able to steam. With sunset they could break off combat and reach Vladivostok.

At 6.40pm, 20 minutes from sunset, Togo got a decisive break. Two 12in. shells from *Asahi* hit *Tsesarevich*. One hit killed Vitgeft and his staff, the second jammed the helm hard over, putting *Tsesarevich* in a hard turn to port. Unaware of the death of the admiral, the rest of the Russian line followed the tight turn and fell into confusion. Vitgeft's second-in-command, Rear Admiral Prince Ukhtomsky aboard *Peresvyet*, took over. However, *Peresvyet*'s mast had been destroyed and no one could read his signals.

The Japanese battle line closed in. The Russian battleship *Retvizan*'s captain, on his own initiative, charged the Japanese line. The single-handed charge saved *Retvizan*. So many shells landed from the concentrated fire of the Japanese that their gunners could not adjust their fire. The badly damaged Japanese battleships, nearly out of 12in. ammunition, fell back as darkness descended.

Ukhtomsky ordered the fleet back to Port Arthur. Five battleships, the cruiser *Pallada* and nine destroyers returned to Port Arthur. *Tsesarevich*, three cruisers and four destroyers were either left behind or took the opportunity to escape in the darkness. *Tsesarevich*, accompanied by three destroyers, limped to the German concession at Tsingtao, where they were interned. The cruiser *Askold* and another destroyer made it to Shanghai, where they too were disarmed and interned. The cruiser *Diana* continued to Saigon, where it was also interned.

Novik was the only Russian ship that refused to return to Port Arthur or accept internment in a neutral port. It attempted to reach Vladivostok through La Perouse Strait. It was detected, and intercepted by two Japanese cruisers. (AC)

Only the cruiser *Novik* resolved to fight on. It stopped at Tsingtao, and loaded as much coal as it could in the hours between its night-time arrival and dawn. Then, fearing it would be blockaded by the Japanese and face internment, it slipped out of harbour, determined to reach Vladivostok.

Novik continued its voyage to Vladivostok, choosing to sail around the Japanese Home Islands and entering the Sea of Japan through the La Perouse Strait. Its engines had been poorly maintained at Port Arthur and its fuel consumption was abnormally high. To reach Vladivostok it needed to refuel. It stopped at Korsakov, a port on the southern tip of Sakhalin Island, eight days after leaving Tsingtao. *Novik* was spotted entering the straits and protected cruisers *Niitaka* and *Tsushima* were dispatched to run down *Novik*.

Coaling took time. *Novik* was loading the last two barges on 20 August when the Japanese arrived. Outnumbered and outgunned, *Novik* attempted to break into the Sea of Japan, but was driven back into Aniva Bay. Damaged, and unable to run, its crew scuttled *Novik* and fled inland. After a long journey, they crossed to the mainland and reached Vladivostok overland.

The Vladivostok Independent Cruiser Squadron received word of Vitgeft's 10 August sortie late the following day. Vice Admiral Karl Jessen, commanding the squadron, originally planned to meet the 1st Pacific Squadron in the Korean Strait if they attempted a breakout. He led his squadron out of Vladivostok as evening fell on 13 August, unaware the bulk of the 1st Pacific Squadron had already returned to Port Arthur. Jessen believed it was too late to meet Vitgeft's ships in the Korean Strait, but hoped to rendezvous in the Sea of Japan.

The Battle of Ulsan.

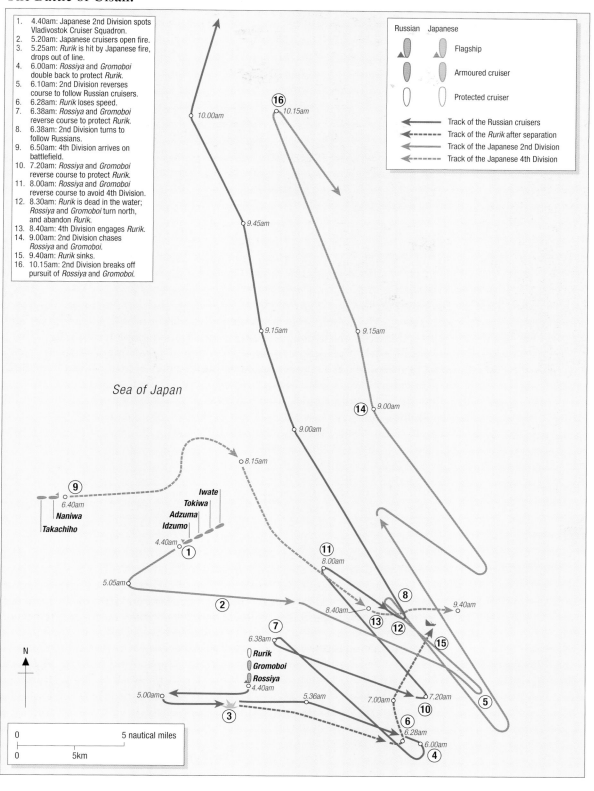

1. 4.40am: Japanese 2nd Division spots Vladivostok Cruiser Squadron.
2. 5.20am: Japanese cruisers open fire.
3. 5.25am: *Rurik* is hit by Japanese fire, drops out of line.
4. 6.00am: *Rossiya* and *Gromoboi* double back to protect *Rurik*.
5. 6.10am: 2nd Division reverses course to follow Russian cruisers.
6. 6.28am: *Rurik* loses speed.
7. 6.38am: *Rossiya* and *Gromoboi* reverse course to protect *Rurik*.
8. 6.38am: 2nd Division turns to follow Russians.
9. 6.50am: 4th Division arrives on battlefield.
10. 7.20am: *Rossiya* and *Gromoboi* reverse course to protect *Rurik*.
11. 8.00am: *Rossiya* and *Gromoboi* reverse course to avoid 4th Division.
12. 8.30am: *Rurik* is dead in the water; *Rossiya* and *Gromoboi* turn north, and abandon *Rurik*.
13. 8.40am: 4th Division engages *Rurik*.
14. 9.00am: 2nd Division chases *Rossiya* and *Gromoboi*.
15. 9.40am: *Rurik* sinks.
16. 10.15am: 2nd Division breaks off pursuit of *Rossiya* and *Gromoboi*.

Russian   Japanese

Flagship

Armoured cruiser

Protected cruiser

Track of the Russian cruisers

Track of the *Rurik* after separation

Track of the Japanese 2nd Division

Track of the Japanese 4th Division

Sea of Japan

10.00am

16 10.15am

9.45am

9.15am   9.15am

14 9.00am

9.00am

8.15am

9 6.40am

Iwate
Tokiwa
Adzuma
Izdumo

Naniwa

Takachiho

4.40am

1

5.05am

2

11
8.00am

8

8.40am   9.40am

13   12

7
6.38am

15

Rurik
Gromoboi
Rossiya
4.40am   5.36am   7.00am   7.20am

N

5.00am

3   6.28am   10   5

6
6.28am

4   6.00am

0   5 nautical miles
0   5km

59

The ships swept as far south as Tsushima. Finding no evidence the Port Arthur ships were around, Jessen turned around after reaching the island and headed home. Vice Admiral Kamimura Hikonojo was patrolling the Sea of Japan with the four armoured cruisers of the 2nd Division (then *Idzumo*, *Adzuma*, *Tokiwa* and *Iwate*) while four protected cruisers were escorting transports from Japan to Korea. The Russian and Japanese armoured cruisers passed each other in the night. As dawn broke, Kamimura's ships were between the Russian cruisers and Vladivostok. Jessen's ships were spotted as they headed north-west, silhouetted against the rising sun.

Kamimura gave chase, concentrating fire on the aftmost (and smallest) Russian cruiser, *Rurik*. Most of *Rurik*'s officers were killed in the running gunfight and the rudder jammed hard over by a hit. Forced to steer by engines, Rurik fell behind. *Rossiya* and *Gromoboi* attempted to draw Kamimura's armoured cruisers away from *Rurik*, but two protected cruisers, *Naniwa* and *Takachiho*, joined the battle, going after *Rurik*. Finally, *Rurik*'s senior surviving officer ordered the sinking *Rurik* scuttled and Jessen ordered the two surviving cruisers to Vladivostok. Although Kamimura's ships had suffered damage, it was relatively minor. Kamimura broke off the action when *Rossiya* and *Gromoboi* fled, allowing them to reach Vladivostok. *Rossiya*, despite the damage it took, was repaired in two months. *Gromoboi* was damaged beyond the capacity of Vladivostok to repair.

Over a ten-day period, the Russian naval presence in the Pacific was effectively destroyed. The Vladivostok Independent Cruiser Squadron was neutralized. The bulk of the 1st Pacific Squadron was trapped in Port Arthur, with the rest interned at neutral ports. The ships in Port Arthur were too weak to fight their way past Togo's blockade. Port Arthur's sole remaining hope of survival lay in reinforcements from Russia's European fleets. Although a 2nd Pacific Squadron was being assembled, in August it had still not sailed.

VOYAGE OF THE BALTIC FLEET, OCTOBER 1904–APRIL 1905

When war broke out in February 1904, there was no immediate call to reinforce the 1st Pacific Squadron at Port Arthur. Russia expected to win the war easily and quickly. Eleven Russian warships were en route to Port

Arthur, including a battleship and two armoured cruisers. Some reached Djibouti at the Horn of Africa before the war started. All were recalled to St Petersburg.

It soon became apparent there would be no quick, easy Russian victory. After Japan cut off Port Arthur on 15 May, calls began to reinforce the 1st Pacific Squadron. On 20 June, the Navy Board with Tsar Nicholas presiding ordered assembly of a 2nd Pacific Squadron to reinforce Port Arthur.

The board selected Vice Admiral Zinovy Rozhestvensky to organize and command the new fleet. Rozhestvensky, a favourite of the Tsar, was an extremely competent organizer. He was given a free hand in selecting the Baltic Fleet ships to be sent and arranging the logistics for the voyage. (Turkey refused to permit Russian Black Sea warships to use the Bosphorus.) He resolved to sail in July.

Rozhestvensky resolved to take only the best ships available. This included four just-completed Borodino-class battleships, the Peresvyet-class battleship *Oslyabya* and two older but still useful battleships, *Sisoi Veliky* and *Navarin*. He added the most modern three armoured cruisers available

plus *Dmitri Donskoi*, launched 21 years earlier. Three modern protected cruisers for scouting and nine destroyers were included. His fleet train had two transports, a repair ship, an ammunition ship, two tugs and two hospital ships escorted by *Almaz*, a combination imperial yacht-scout cruiser.

Oslyabya, the cruisers *Aurora* and *Dmitri Donskoi* and five destroyers were the ships travelling to Port Arthur in February. They were fully manned and ready for sea. The rest of the ships were unready. Only one Borodino-class battleship was in commission in June. The rest were nearing completion. *Oryel* was finally commissioned in October. Ships had to fill out undermanned crews. Their most experienced sailors were sent to Port Arthur when the war opened to fill out Pacific Fleet crews. Spares and supplies were also short and requests were filled ineptly and late.

Rozhestvensky's July sailing date passed without the fleet departing. It was unready to sail in August, when the naval disasters on the Yellow Sea and Sea of Japan made the need for reinforcements urgent. In September, he did manage to get the fleet to Libau, 450 nautical miles from St Petersburg's naval base of Kronstadt. The 2nd Pacific Squadron finally left Russian waters on 16 October 1905.

Getting a 31-ship Russian fleet to sea in just four months – a monumental task – was dwarfed by the challenge of getting it to the Pacific. Ships were fuelled by coal, a low-energy fuel, requiring frequent renewal. It was heavy and hard to handle. International law prevented warships from refuelling in a neutral port beyond the minimums necessary to get them to the nearest

Sending the 2nd Pacific Squadron required fuelling it along the route. Neutrality laws prevented belligerent warships from fuelling in neutral ports. Instead, arrangements were made to re-coal at sea, using a network of colliers leased from German-registered companies. (AC)

Route of the 2nd and 3rd Pacific Squadrons.

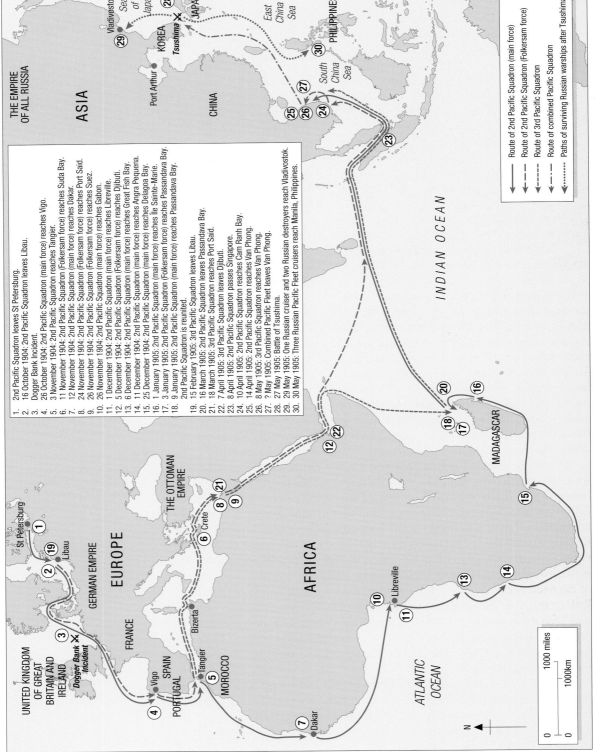

1. 2nd Pacific Squadron leaves St Petersburg.
2. 16 October 1904: 2nd Pacific Squadron leaves Libau.
3. Dogger Bank Incident.
4. 26 October 1904: 2nd Pacific Squadron (main force) reaches Vigo.
5. 3 November 1904: 2nd Pacific Squadron reaches Tangier.
6. 11 November 1904: 2nd Pacific Squadron (Folkersam force) reaches Suda Bay.
7. 12 November 1904: 2nd Pacific Squadron (main force) reaches Dakar.
8. 24 November 1904: 2nd Pacific Squadron (Folkersam force) reaches Port Said.
9. 26 November 1904: 2nd Pacific Squadron (Folkersam force) reaches Suez.
10. 26 November 1904: 2nd Pacific Squadron (main force) reaches Gabon.
11. 1 December 1904: 2nd Pacific Squadron (main force) reaches Libreville.
12. 5 December 1904: 2nd Pacific Squadron (Folkersam force) reaches Djibuti.
13. 6 December 1904: 2nd Pacific Squadron (main force) reaches Great Fish Bay.
14. 11 December 1904: 2nd Pacific Squadron (main force) reaches Angra Pequena.
15. 25 December 1904: 2nd Pacific Squadron (main force) reaches Delagoa Bay.
16. 1 January 1905: 2nd Pacific Squadron (main force) reaches Île Sainte-Marie.
17. 3 January 1905: 2nd Pacific Squadron (Folkersam force) reaches Passandava Bay.
18. 9 January 1905: 2nd Pacific Squadron (main force) reaches Passandava Bay. 2nd Pacific Squadron is reunited.
19. 15 February 1905: 3rd Pacific Squadron leaves Libau.
20. 16 March 1905: 2nd Pacific Squadron leaves Passandava Bay.
21. 18 March 1905: 3rd Pacific Squadron reaches Port Said.
22. 7 April 1905: 3rd Pacific Squadron leaves Djibuti.
23. 8 April 1905: 2nd Pacific Squadron passes Singapore.
24. 10 April 1905: 2nd Pacific Squadron reaches Cam Ranh Bay.
25. 14 April 1905: 2nd Pacific Squadron reaches Van Phong.
26. 8 May 1905: 3rd Pacific Squadron reaches Van Phong.
27. ? May 1905: Combined Pacific Fleet leaves Van Phong.
28. 27 May 1905: Battle of Tsushima.
29. 29 May 1905: One Russian cruiser and two Russian destroyers reach Vladivostok.
30. 30 May 1905: Three Russian Pacific Fleet cruisers reach Manila, Philippines.

Route of 2nd Pacific Squadron (main force)

Route of 2nd Pacific Squadron (Folkersam force)

Route of 3rd Pacific Squadron

Route of combined Pacific Squadron

Paths of surviving Russian warships after Tsushima

friendly port. Great Britain, allied with Japan but neutral, insisted on the strictest adherence to this, making it impossible for Rozhestvensky's fleet to coal in ports controlled by Britain or its allies.

Germany and France, although neutral, were friendly with Russia. Germany allowed Russia to charter German colliers to carry coal, and France – with neutral nations like Spain and Tangiers – tolerated Russian ships anchoring in port roadsteads, i.e. outside a port but sheltered. Rozhestvensky would re-coal at sea. The trip from St Petersburg to Port Arthur was over 17,000 nautical miles. His ships had to refuel once every 2,500 nautical miles. Thus, Rozhestvensky needed at least seven successful coaling stops to reach Port Arthur.

There was a range of behaviours a nation could observe in maintaining neutrality, and an officially impartial, passive Britain improved Rozhestvensky's chances. He could survive closed British ports and being refused resupply, and could even survive Britain serving as an unofficial intelligence service for Japan, reporting Russia's progress. However, a neutral Britain actively hostile to Russia and exerting diplomatic pressure on other neutral nations to follow strict neutrality could make it impossible for him to finish his voyage. Britain as a Japanese co-belligerent imperilled the survival of his fleet. Four days after leaving Libau, the 2nd Pacific Squadron brought Britain to the brink of war with Russia.

Once the Russian fleet left harbour, it was dogged by imagined Japanese activity. Green crews saw illusionary observation balloons, manned by Japanese observers intent on monitoring Russian progress. Rumours swept the fleet of Japanese torpedo boats hidden in secret Scandinavian bases ready to head out at night to torpedo Russian battleships, as they had done at Port Arthur. Non-existent minefields were evaded. As the fleet passed into the North Sea, everyone was on edge. That night, Rozhestvensky steamed well north of normal sea lanes to the English Channel, possibly to throw off non-existent pursuers.

As the fleet plunged through darkness, the repair ship *Kamchatka* reported being attacked by torpedo boats. No other ship saw these attackers, but all ships went to battle stations. Searchlights swept the waters. Suddenly, lights of many small vessels appeared. One of the Russian vessels fired, followed by another. Finally, most of the warships fired at the lights of the unknown ships. Russian vessels were hit by wild shots, reinforcing the impression the fleet was under attack.

The unknown vessels were the Hull fishing fleet. Eventually, the Russians satisfied themselves that no Japanese torpedo boats remained hidden among the fishing boats, and they ceased firing. By then, one trawler had been sunk and four others damaged. Two Russians were dead and others seriously wounded by mislaid Russian gunfire.

The next day, war fever swept Britain, its citizens incensed at the unprovoked attack on British civilians. The British Home Fleet, 28 battleships strong, raised steam and prepared for action. The Russians passed through the English Channel shadowed by Royal Navy cruisers. Tsar Nicholas, unwilling to fight with both Japan and Britain, ordered his fleet to stop at Vigo and disembark the officers considered most responsible. They would testify at an international commission established to investigate. Rozhestvensky continued to insist Japanese torpedo boats were hiding among the fishing boats.

After refuelling in Vigo, Rozhestvensky took his fleet to Tangier, then still independent. *Kamchatka* got separated from the rest of the fleet. It arrived at Tangier with tales of fighting off more Japanese torpedo boats – in reality three neutral merchantmen. *Kamchatka* fired 300 rounds, which all missed. Rozhestvensky split the fleet at Tangier, sending the destroyers, the two oldest battleships and weakest three cruisers through the Mediterranean and Red Sea. The rest of the fleet sailed around Africa. The two parts would rendezvous at Madagascar.

Why did he not move all ships through the Suez route? The official reason was he feared the new battleships were too big to fit in the canal. Perhaps Rozhestvensky worried Britain might intern the Russian fleet once in the

Suez Canal and was unwilling to risk his newest warships. Alternatively, he feared possible attacks by Japanese torpedo boats in the narrow waters of the Mediterranean and Red seas. Regardless, after the older and weaker ships sailed east under the command of Rear Admiral Dmitry von Folkersam, Rozhestvensky took the main body west, for a voyage around the Cape of Good Hope.

The trip began inauspiciously. An auxiliary raising its anchor snagged and snapped Tangier's telegraph cable, severing European communications for four days. Rozhestvensky's ships went around Africa, stopping at Dakar, Gabon, Libreville, Great Fish Bay and Angra Pequena on Africa's Atlantic coast. Avoiding a stop at the British Cape Colony, it rounded the Cape of Good Hope making a non-stop voyage to Île Sainte-Marie in Madagascar.

The fleet's stops were made at ports in French, Portuguese and German colonies. Germany and Portugal were officially blind when the Russians arrived. France wished to avoid irritating Britain. Spaced seven days to two weeks apart for refuelling, the stops followed a pattern. The Russians anchored, rendezvoused with colliers and fuelled. After a day in port, French port authorities demanded Rozhestvensky depart or risk internment. Rozhestvensky ignored these demands until they had finished coaling. Overloaded with coal (because Rozhestvensky could never be sure he could ignore the next demands to depart) the fleet left. Port officials then duly informed Paris the Russians had departed, as demanded.

The voyage was miserable. Coal was stored everywhere, coal dust pervasive and the Russian crews, brought up in northern Russia, faced equatorial heat as the fleet sailed down Africa's Atlantic coast and turbulent seas of the Roaring Forties as they rounded Africa to head to Madagascar. Meanwhile, conditions in Port Arthur were deteriorating.

By September, the Russians had retreated to the hills immediately around Port Arthur, with the Japanese lines only five miles from the naval port. By 16 October, when Rozhestvensky arrived at Dakar, the Japanese were assaulting those hills. By 1 December, when the 2nd Pacific Squadron was at Libreville, the Japanese had taken 203 Metre Hill, the key to Port Arthur's

The 3rd Pacific Squadron was sent to reinforce Rozhestvensky, largely at the urging of Captain Nikolai Klado, who wrote a series of articles urging their dispatch. It was made up of ships previously rejected for service by Rozhestvensky. (AC)

THE ATTACK ON THE HULL FISHING FLEET (PP. 66–67)

Dogger Bank had been a fishing ground for centuries. It was one of Britain's major sources for herring from which kippers, beloved at British breakfast tables, were made. Herring swam in huge schools so it was more efficient to harvest them with fleets of small trawlers working together. At the start of the 20th century, Hull was the port from which these ships operated. The Gamecock Fleet, as it was known, would steam from Hull to Dogger Bank and stay for days. Four dozen fishing trawlers, six carriers (ships that took the catch from the trawlers and ran them to port) and a hospital ship were a standard fleet.

The ships (1) were small. They carried crews of five. The steam-powered trawlers were 80–90ft long, with a 20ft beam. The trawlers would fish as long as the herring were schooling, often through the night. The fish were dressed on the trawler and sent to a carrier by boat for the trip to Hull. They were also well lit. Big steamers were supposed to avoid the fishing boats. When the ships of the 2nd Pacific Squadron (2) blundered into the Hull trawlers, most of those aboard the Gamecock Fleet probably ignored them: the trawler crews (3) were focused on their work. Everyone knew about the herring fleet – except the keyed-up Russians.

The crews of the Russian warships had been expecting an attack since leaving Libau. It made little sense, but panic rarely does. The *Kamchatka* reported it was being attacked by Japanese torpedo boats, although none apparently had fired on

Kamchatka yet. Then, unexpectedly, the lights of the Gamecock Fleet appeared. There were lots of small boats – like a flotilla of Japanese torpedo boats. Although a herring trawler was two-thirds the length of a naval torpedo boat of the era, it was night, and size could not be judged.

All it took was one trigger-happy gun commander to fire his weapon. Then someone else, hearing the shot, fired back. Searchlights went on, illuminating targets. Soon every gunner was convinced the fleet was being attacked. The wild firing hit other Russian ships, completing the illusion the fleet was under attack. *Aurora* had its chaplain killed by 'friendly fire'.

Although the Russian gunnery was bad, five fishing trawlers were hit, and one sank. Two fishermen died that night, one died later and five were wounded. Even for those in vessels untouched by Russian artillery (Russian accuracy was awful), it was a terrifying experience. The Gamecock Fleet crews found the air filled with flying shells. One minute they were peacefully trawling, the next they found themselves illuminated by a warship searchlight – the target of live artillery. Brave men signalled the Russians, trying to identify themselves as innocent fishermen. Sensible men threw themselves on deck, preferably with something metal and thick between them and the incoming shells.

From the perspective of the fishermen, the chaos must have seemed like the world was ending.

Rozhestvensky attempted to elude the 3rd Pacific Squadron by sailing from Madagascar before the 3rd Squadron arrived. Its location was unknown to the world for the next three weeks until it reached the Straits of Malacca, as shown, on 8 April. (AC)

defences. Before it reached Angra Pequena, on 11 December, Japanese siege guns had sunk every major warship in Port Arthur, except the battleship *Sevastopol*, anchored in the roadstead to avoid the Japanese Army's artillery. Rozhestvensky reached Madagascar on 29 December. A week later, on 5 January 1905, Port Arthur surrendered.

Folkersam's ships were missing when Rozhestvensky arrived. Rozhestvensky discovered they were at Nosy Be, a harbour on the north-east tip of Madagascar, having been re-routed by Admiralty orders. Expecting Port Arthur to fall, the Admiralty decided to reinforce Rozhestvensky. A 3rd Pacific Squadron made up of obsolete warships Rozhestvensky had previously rejected was sent. Rozhestvensky was ordered to await their arrival at Nosy Be and refit his ships there.

Rozhestvensky went to Nosy Be, intending to reunite his fleet and leave. Instead, shortly after arriving at Nosy Be and starting the process of resupplying and refuelling, Rozhestvensky collapsed, ill. Without Rozhestvensky's drive, preparations halted. He did not recover until late February. Rozhestvensky then resigned, but St Petersburg rejected it. He resumed preparations, convincing the German colliers to accompany him as far as French Indo-China. Without waiting for his 'reinforcements', Rozhestvensky's ships left Nosy Be on 16 March.

The fleet crossed the Indian Ocean, and went unspotted until opposite Singapore. Realizing his only chance to reach Vladivostok depended on speed, Rozhestvensky intended to proceed to Vladivostok without refuelling. When one of his battleships reported it lacked the coal to reach Vladivostok, Rozhestvensky was forced to stop at Cam Ranh Bay in French Indo-China on 14 April.

There, in communication with his admiralty for the first time since leaving Madagascar, Rozhestvensky was ordered to wait for the 3rd Pacific Squadron. He had little choice, as he had to arrange for more coal. France, under pressure from Japan and Britain, ordered Rozhestvensky's ships out. They left, but then anchored at Van Phong out of sight, a few miles north. There he waited. On 9 May, the reinforcements, commanded by Rear Admiral Nikolai Nebogatov, finally arrived. Five days later the combined forces – now entitled the Pacific Fleet – sailed north.

TSUSHIMA: THE APPROACH

Rozhestvensky was correct when he assumed speed was the 2nd Pacific Squadron's ally and time its enemy. The pauses at Madagascar and Indo-China would prove fatal to the Russians. When Port Arthur surrendered, the Combined Fleet was virtually a spent force. Eleven months' hard service in the storm-tossed Yellow Sea had left its ships badly worn. Battle damage had been repaired hastily, ships' guns were worn out through constant use and maintenance of machinery had been minimal. Running the engines of ships of that era wore them down under normal conditions, and Togo's ships had been run hard since the previous February.

Now Togo had to face a new Russian fleet, as he saw it, filled with battleships fresh out of the builders' yards. With Port Arthur gone and the Vladivostok fleet too damaged to count, Togo could finally get his ships refitted. He rushed the key units of his fleet to Japanese dockyards.

The worn gun barrels were replaced. Machinery received dockyard overhauls, broken equipment was fixed or replaced, and hasty repairs redone. The process took months. Had Rozhestvensky left Madagascar on 15 January and plunged on to Vladivostok with only a pause for refuelling off French Indo-China, the 1st Pacific Squadron would have been passing the Tsushima Strait in late March, well before this work was completed. The Russians would have faced no more than three Japanese battleships. *Asahi* had been mined in November and repairs were not completed until mid-April. Other ships, including one or more battleships and cruisers, did not complete their refits until late April.

At the start of May, the work was complete. The delayed departure of the Russians from Van Phong gave Togo several weeks to shake down his fleet. Rozhestvensky faced a refurbished foe with veteran crews and the confidence that winning hard-fought battles gave the Japanese.

Asahi struck a mine off Port Arthur on 26 October 1904. Repairs were completed only in late April 1905. Had the Russian fleet not delayed waiting for reinforcements, *Asahi* would have been unavailable. (USNHHC)

Russian routes to Vladivostok.

Direct routes
—————— Via Tsushima Strait
— · — · — Via La Perouse Strait
·········· Via Tsugaru Strait

Indirect routes
—————— To Bonin Islands
— · — · — Bonin Islands to Vladivostok via La Perouse Strait
— · — · — Bonin Islands to Vladivostok via Tsugaru Strait
— — — — Bonin Islands to Petropavlovsk-Kamchatsky
·········· Petropavlovsk to Vladivostok via La Perouse Strait
·········· Petropavlovsk to Vladivostok around Sakhalin Island

RUSSIA

SIBERIA

MANCHURIA

MONGOLIA

Sakhalin Island

Petropavlovsk-Kamchatsky

2,600NM

1,900NM

La Perouse Strait

Amur

Vladivostok

Tsugaru Strait

Peking

Port Arthur

KOREA

Sea of Japan

Wei-hai-wei

Kiau-chau

Yellow Sea

JAPAN   Tokyo

1,600NM

2,100NM

2,200NM

Yellow

CHINA

Shanghai

Yangtse

Tsushima Strait

East China Sea

2,100NM

2,800NM
3,300NM

Bonin Islands (Chichi-jima)

Xi (Si-kiang)

Formosa

Hong Kong

2,100NM

PACIFIC

OCEAN

Hainan

ANNAM   PHILIPPINES

0   500 miles

0   500km

The Russians, in theory, had several ways to reach Vladivostok. They could have approached directly via the Tsushima, Tsugau, or La Perouse straits. More extreme possibilities included seizing Chichi-jima in the Bonin Islands and using that for a refuelling stop. From there Rozhestvesky could have used either the Tsugaru or La Perouse straits and had a healthy reserve of coal, or he could have made another refuelling stop at Petropavlovsk-Kamchatsky.

Any of these choices would have confounded Togo's strategy of waiting north of the Tsushima Strait. The direct routes through Tsugaru, or La Perouse were limited by fuel considerations, while seizing the Bonin Islands had been made obsolete by wireless: a warning from the Bonins would have invalidated the strategy. Moreover, any plan other than the most direct route via Tsushima Strait would have likely failed due to the increasing unreliability of the maintenance-desperate Russian warships. Ultimately, Rozhestvesky did what he had to do – and what Togo expected.

Captain Nikolai Klado sailed with the 2nd Pacific Squadron, assigned to Rozhestvensky's staff. He was put ashore at Vigo to testify at the Dogger Bank Commission. Klado wrote a series of articles persuasively arguing for reinforcement of Rozhestvensky's fleet. (AC)

Still worse, the militarily useless reinforcements of the 3rd Pacific Squadron slowed the Russian fleet. *Imperator Nikolai I* had a top speed of only 14 knots on builder's trials in 1890. The three Admiral Ushakov-class coastal defence ships could, in theory, make 16 knots in sheltered waters such as the Baltic Sea. In the open ocean they barely made 10 knots without swamping.

The Russian ships were in poor shape. They had travelled nearly 16,000 nautical miles. During that time they had seen neither a dockyard nor harbour facilities. Only the most basic maintenance that could be done aboard ship by its crew had been carried out. There was a shortage of spares to replace parts worn out from long usage. No gunnery practice had been conducted. Since ammunition could not be replaced, it could not be expended except in combat.

What Rozhestvensky needed most before facing the Combined Fleet was to put his ships through proper dockyard refits, preferably in dry dock where their bottoms could be cleaned, patched and repainted. Giving his crews a week or two of shore leave – which their Japanese counterparts had enjoyed while their ships were refitting, waiting for the arrival of the Russians – would also help. The closest place to do that was Vladivostok with the Japanese fleet between his ships and succor. The question was how to get there.

The shortest route went through the Tsushima Strait, between Korea and Japan. Sailing through the Luzon Strait and the gap between the Miyako and Ryukyu Island chains, the Russians could escape detection until just before they reached the Tsushima Strait. If they neared Tsushima at dusk, with a little luck and some friendly fog, they might slip through undetected. Once in the Sea of Japan between the Combined Fleet and Vladivostok, the Russians could beat the Japanese fleet to Vladivostok.

There were other routes. Instead of going through the Tsushima Strait, Rozhestvensky could have used the Tsugaru or La Perouse straits. The distance from Van Phong to Vladivostok via the Tsugaru Strait was around 2,800 miles. Taking the La Perouse Strait (the route *Novik* had taken) required 3,300 nautical miles of non-stop steaming. In either case, the Pacific Fleet would be detected entering those straits. However, if Togo's ships were waiting near the Tsushima Strait, Tsugaru Strait was two days' steaming and the La Perouse Strait three days' steaming.

Even assuming the Russians were discovered on the Pacific side of the strait, Togo would be lucky to catch Rozhestvensky before the Russians reached Vladivostok. If Togo immediately raised steam and headed directly to Vladivostok, it would take anywhere from 54 to 60 hours to leave harbour, form up and steam to Vladivostok. From the Pacific entrance of the Tsugaru Strait to Vladivostok was only 46 hours' steaming. If Rozhestvensky did not dawdle, the last of the Russian ships would be tying up in harbour before Togo arrived.

Two factors argued against this course. The first was the risk. It assumed Togo would be waiting near the Tsushima Strait. If word of the attempt leaked out, or if a neutral merchantman encountered the Russian fleet steaming up the Japanese coast, Togo would be waiting outside the exit. Then Rozhestvensky would have to fight the Combined Fleet with barely enough fuel to reach Vladivostok at a 9-knot cruising speed.

The second factor was the ships of the 3rd Pacific Squadron. The Admiral Ushakov-class ships were designed to operate in the confined waters of the Baltic. The bunkers of two of them held a bare 400 tons of coal, while the third only carried 330 tons. This was enough to get them from Van Phong to Vladivostok via the direct route, but not much more. They officially had a range of 3,000 nautical miles. Given aged engines worn from a long voyage, it was unlikely they could steam 2,800 miles without requiring a tow for the last leg.

Another possibility, advocated after the war by Nikolai Klado, would be for Rozhestvensky to take his fleet (with the German colliers), capture the Bonin Islands and use these as a secret base of operation. From the Bonin Islands it was only 1,600 nautical miles to Vladivostok via the Tsugaru Strait and 2,100 using the La Perouse Strait. Alternatively, from the Bonins Rozhestvensky could have gone to Petropavlovsk-Kamchatsky, refuelled in that port and then slipped around Sakhalin Island to Vladivostok.

It might have worked in 1895, before the widespread introduction of radio: secrecy was paramount for this to work. A radioed report from the island that it was under attack would reveal Russian presence. It also underestimated the difficulty Rozhestvensky would have convincing the neutral Germans to bring colliers into a war zone and then convincing the colliers to remain to maintain secrecy. It sounded great on paper, but was unworkable in practice.

Rozhestvensky took the only practical course available: through the Tsushima Strait to Vladivostok. He planned to time his arrival to pass through the strait at night and hope he was not spotted. Coal was loaded and the colliers dismissed. Rozhestvensky's distain for the 3rd Pacific Squadron ships was so great he issued no orders other than to follow him. He did not keep Nebogatov informed of his plans, even though Nebogatov was the combined force's third-ranking officer; Rozhestvensky's second-in-command, Folkersam, was dying. Even after Folkersam died, the day before the battle, Nebogatov was not informed.

Rozhestvensky's gamble almost worked. The fleet arrived near the Goto Islands at the entrance of the Strait, before being spotted. Togo had a screen of four armed merchant cruisers screening the 100-mile gap between Jeju and the Goto Islands: *Shinano Maru*, *America Maru*, *Sado Maru* and *Manshu Maru*. Then, about 4.00am on 27 May, *Shinano Maru* spotted a ship signalling in the fog-covered seas. It was the hospital ship *Orel* trailing the Russian fleet. *Shinano Maru* closed, and discovered warships beyond the seeming merchant ship. Before the Russians could react, *Shinano Maru* disappeared into the fog and radioed a message to Togo's fleet.

In 1905, Petropavlovsk was a very minor port on the Kamchatka Peninsula. It lacked the coal reserves to refuel Rozhestvensky's fleet. That did not prevent armchair admirals from arguing Rozhestvensky would have avoided defeat if he had attempted to refuel. (AC)

The Tsushima Strait.

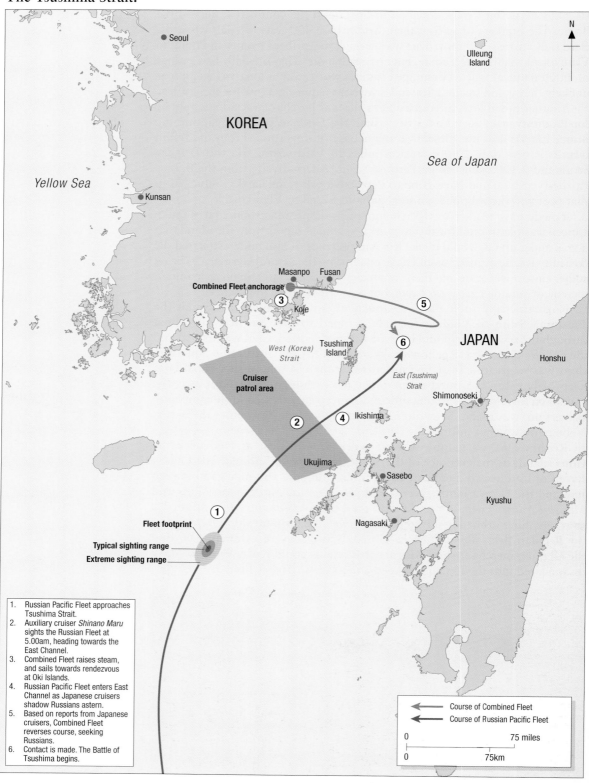

N

Seoul

Ulleung
Island

KOREA

Sea of Japan

Yellow Sea

Kunsan

Masanpo Fusan

Combined Fleet anchorage

③

Koje

West (Korea)
Strait

Tsushima
Island

⑤

⑥

JAPAN

Honshu

**Cruiser
patrol area**

East (Tsushima)
Strait

Shimonoseki

② ④ Ikishima

Ukujima

Sasebo

Kyushu

Nagasaki

Fleet footprint ①

Typical sighting range

Extreme sighting range

1. Russian Pacific Fleet approaches
   Tsushima Strait.
2. Auxiliary cruiser *Shinano Maru*
   sights the Russian Fleet at
   5.00am, heading towards the
   East Channel.
3. Combined Fleet raises steam,
   and sails towards rendezvous
   at Oki Islands.
4. Russian Pacific Fleet enters East
   Channel as Japanese cruisers
   shadow Russians astern.
5. Based on reports from Japanese
   cruisers, Combined Fleet
   reverses course, seeking
   Russians.
6. Contact is made. The Battle of
   Tsushima begins.

Course of Combined Fleet
Course of Russian Pacific Fleet

0   75 miles

0   75km

TSUSHIMA: THE FIRST DAY

Togo stationed his fleet at Busan in Korea, awaiting the arrival of the Russian fleet. After Rozhestvensky dismissed the colliers and set out into the South China Sea, several colliers steamed to Shanghai for reassignment. Japanese intelligence was able to determine the time and point of Rozhestvensky's departure. Togo correctly guessed Rozhestvensky's route (and could perform the same fuel-consumption calculations as Rozhestvensky). He set up a patrol line south of the Tsushima Strait using armed merchant cruisers. Lightly armed, fast and equipped with powerful radios, they allowed Togo to deploy a far-reaching patrol line without significantly weakening the combat power of his fleet.

Togo assumed a 10-knot cruising speed for the Russians. Rozhestvensky, plagued by slow ships, actually made 9 knots, making their arrival the day after Togo expected their appearance, during the evening of 25/26 May. If *Orel* had been a little closer to the main body of the fleet or not used its signal lamps, *Shinano Maru* might have missed the Russians entirely. Having found them, it kept in touch, following as the Russian fleet moved up the wider eastern strait.

Once Togo received word of the Russians' arrival, he ordered his fleet to sea. His ships' boilers were hot. They raised steam, moving out of Busan with the 1st Division, headed by *Mikasa* leading the way. It was followed by the armoured cruisers of Kamimura's 2nd Division. Initially the ships steamed almost due east, heading for a prearranged rendezvous near Mishima, a small island off Honshu. The cruiser divisions were sent after the Russians. The first cruiser to spot them was the ancient *Izumi*, launched in 1883 and purchased by Japan in 1894. After briefly making contact off the Russians' port side at 7.00am, it fell back into the fog.

Soon, three Japanese cruiser divisions lined up to the left of the Russian fleet. Kataoka's 5th Division, with the elderly prize battleship *Chinyen* and three old and eccentric Matsushima-class cruisers. They were followed by Rear Admiral Togo Masamichi's 6th Division, less *Izumi*, sailing independently of the three elderly cruisers under this Togo's command.

Togo held the Combined Fleet in Busan, Korea, with full bunkers and the boilers lit, expecting Rozhestvensky. Once word the Russians were approaching the strait arrived, Togo's ships raised steam, with *Mikasa* leading the left to meet the Russian fleet. (AC)

Tsushima: the first day's action.

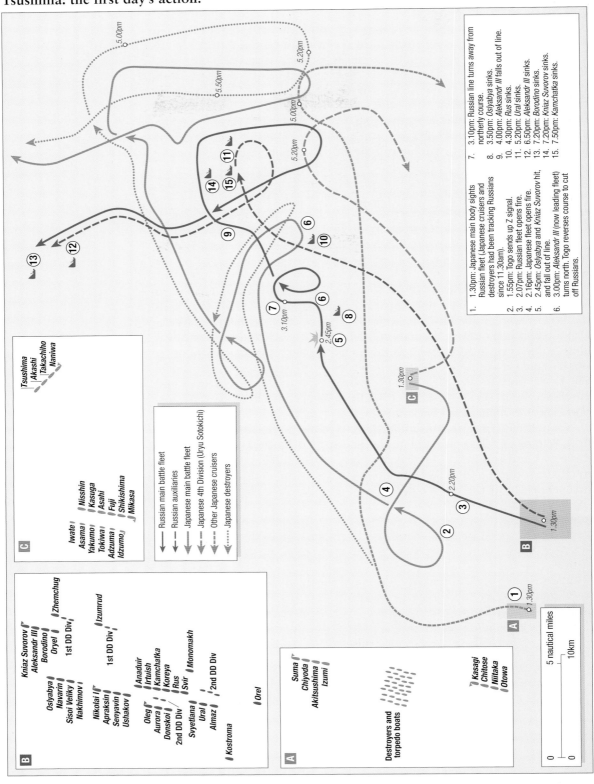

1. 1.30pm: Japanese main body sights Russian fleet (Japanese cruisers and destroyers had been tracking Russians since 11.30am).
2. 1.55pm: Togo sends up Z signal.
3. 2.07pm: Russian fleet opens fire.
4. 2.16pm: Japanese fleet opens fire.
5. 2.45pm: Oslyabya and Kniaz Suvorov hit, and fall out of line.
6. 3.00pm: Aleksandr III (now leading fleet) turns north. Togo reverses course to cut off Russians.
7. 3.10pm: Russian line turns away from northerly course.
8. 3.50pm: Oslyabya sinks.
9. 4.00pm: Aleksandr III falls out of line.
10. 4.30pm: Rus sinks.
11. 5.20pm: Ural sinks.
12. 6.50pm: Aleksandr III sinks.
13. 7.20pm: Borodino sinks.
14. 7.20pm: Kniaz Suvorov sinks.
15. 7.50pm: Kamchatka sinks.

C
Iwate | Nisshin
Asama | Kasuga
Yakumo | Asahi
Tokiwa | Fuji
Idzumo | Shikishima
| Mikasa

Tsushima | Akashi | Takachiho | Naniwa

— Russian main battle fleet
— Russian auxiliaries
— Japanese main battle fleet
— Japanese 4th Division (Uryu Sotokichi)
— Other Japanese cruisers
⋯⋯ Japanese destroyers

B
Kniaz Suvorov
Aleksandr III
Oryel | Zhemchug
Borodino | 1st DD Div
Oslyabya | Izumrud
Navarin
Sisoi Veliky | 1st DD Div
Nakhimov
Nikolai I | Anaduir
Apraksin | Irtuish
Senyavin | Kamchatka
Ushakov | Koreya
Oleg | Rus
Aurora | Svir | Monomakh
Donskoi | 2nd DD Div
2nd DD Div | Syetlana
Ural
Almaz | 2nd DD Div

Orel

Kostroma

A
Suma
Chiyoda
Izumi
Akitsushima

Destroyers and
torpedo boats

Kasagi
Chitose
Niitaka
Otowa

5 nautical miles
0
10km
0

Dewa, with four protected cruisers – *Kasagi, Chitose, Otowa* and *Niitaka* – trailed behind. (*Otowa* and *Niitaka* replaced *Takasago* and *Yoshino* sunk earlier in the war.) They paralleled the Russian fleet, just out of range throughout the morning.

Rozhestvensky did not attack the shadowing cruisers, plunging doggedly ahead. His ships cleared for action. Then, because it was the anniversary of the Tsar and Tsarina's coronation, a thanksgiving service was held. At the midday meal, an extra tot of vodka was served out to the men in celebration. Except for an exchange of fire between *Vladimir Monomakh* and several Japanese destroyers at about 11.00am, both sides continued ahead silently.

Until noon, Rozhestvensky had his fleet in rough line ahead, with the three divisions of battleships following one after another, the cruisers behind Nebogatov's division and the auxiliaries parallelling the cruisers on their starboard side. Then Rozhestvensky ordered a 90-degree turn in succession. When more Japanese cruisers appeared ahead of him, he cancelled the course change, just after his 1st Division completed the turn and then resumed his original course. This resulted in the 1st Division having the four Borodino-class battleships in a line to the right of and only partially ahead of the four older battleships of the 2nd Division. It was his second and last command of the day.

Just then, emerging from the mists ahead of the leading Russian ship were Togo's 1st and 2nd divisions in parallel lines: Togo's four battleships and armoured cruisers *Kasuga* and *Nisshin* in the column to the left, with Kamimura Hikonojo's six armoured cruisers on the right. Togo had been tracking the Russian fleet from his cruisers' reports. He turned from his eastward course to the south-west with his ships in position to intercept Rozhestvensky's fleet as it headed to Vladivostok. At 1.36pm, the two sets of battleships sighted each other.

At 1.40pm, Togo turned his ships starboard to cut across the Russian line. He then raised the famous 'Z' signal: 'The rise or fall of the Empire depends upon the result of this engagement; do your utmost, every one of you.' As Togo's ships crossed the Russian line, the leading Russian ships fired ranging shots with secondary batteries.

The Combined Fleet fought Tsushima as a well-drilled and experienced force. Despite effective Russian fire at the battle's onset, the Japanese never lost discipline, absorbing the initial damage and going on to defeat the Russian battle line. (AC)

Once past the Russian line, Togo made a 270-degree turn to port. Kamimura's division slid in behind the battleships. Both fleets were sailing on parallel courses. At 2.20pm, both fleets opened fire. Initially, the Japanese concentrated fire on *Kniaz Suvorov*, *Oslyabya* (the division flagships) and *Imperator Alexandr III*, immediately behind *Suvorov*. Nebogatov's division was initially ignored. The Russians appear to have fired at the ships opposite them, as most of the leading Japanese ships were hit during the opening phase.

At first Russian fire was excellent. *Mikasa* was hit 15 times in the first five minutes of fire. This was half the total hits it would receive all day. *Shikishima* was also hit. Three of *Kasuga*'s guns were put out of action. *Nisshin* took several hits; fragments of one struck a junior officer aboard, severing two fingers from Isoroku Yamamoto's left hand. (Had he lost another finger, he would have been medically disqualified from further service. Instead, he would rise to command the Combined Fleet in World War II.) *Adzuma* lost one of its four 8in. guns after being struck by a 12in. shell.

Then, Japanese shells began hitting the Russians. The Japanese fire was faster and more accurate than that of the Russians, and the Japanese shells, filled with Shimose powder, did more damage when they struck. Russian gunnery accuracy fell off. *Oslyabya*, older and less protected than the Borodino-class ships, was the first to go. Under concentrated fire from two battleships and two armoured cruisers, it fell out of line and sank at 3.10pm, carrying Folkersam's body with it. He had died three days earlier, but his death was kept secret.

Kniaz Suvorov fell out of line at around the same time, after its steering was hit. It was tougher, though, surviving another four hours before sinking, receiving several poundings by the Japanese fleet whenever it sailed past the crippled flagship. Rozhestvensky was badly injured during this period. When the Russian destroyer *Buini* happened past the disabled flagship, Rozhestvensky's chief of staff and aide transferred their unconscious leader to it. They gave *Buini*'s captain orders to run Rozhestvensky to Vladivostok. *Buini*, overloaded with survivors from *Oslyabya*, promptly obeyed the order.

With the two flagships out of action, command should have gone to Nebogatov. In the middle of the battle this was impractical. The captain of *Imperator Alexandr III* directed the battle line. It and the *Borodino*, the battleship immediately behind it, now received the concentrated fire of the Japanese 1st Division. Conditions were foggy and after 90 minutes' fighting, the fog mixed with smoke. *Imperator Alexandr III* turned away from the Japanese battle line and disappeared into the mists. The Japanese lost contact, regained contact and resumed firing. The Russian battle line would make several looping turns to the south and east, but could not escape Togo's battleships.

Kasuga (shown) and *Nisshin* replaced the two Japanese battleships lost to mines in the First Fleet's 1st Division. Both armoured cruisers mounted a single 10in. gun forward. Other than the 12in. guns of the four battleships, these were the largest guns carried by modern Japanese warships. (USNHHC)

Finally, around 5.00pm, still hours from sunset in a long, late May day, the Russians turned north-west. By then, Nebogatov had finally been advised he commanded the fleet, when the destroyer *Buini* closed with *Imperator Nikolai I*, Nebogatov's flagship, to tell him Rozhestvensky was unconscious. The only strategy then left was to pound towards Vladivostok and hope night would fall before the Japanese sank all the Russians.

The Russian cruisers broke off from the battle line early in the action, before firing began. Led by *Oleg*, flagship of the 1st Cruiser Division commanded by Rear Admiral Oskar Enkvist, the cruisers formed a separate line with the Russian battleships between the cruisers and the Japanese battle line. Soon every cruiser bar three joined Enkvist's line; *Almaz* and *Ural* stayed with the auxiliaries they were assigned to protect, while *Izumrud* fell in at the end of Nebogatov's ships.

Enkvist was a political admiral, assigned over the heads of more senior admirals. He proved his survival skills extended to the battlefield as much as the Admiralty offices. His ships slid around the battlefield avoiding attention from the Japanese battleships and armoured cruisers and he manoeuvred his ships where the Japanese protected cruisers were not. What Enkvist did not do was protect the auxiliaries – his primary responsibility. *Oleg* and *Aurora* took superstructure damage during the day, but nothing that impaired their speed. *Dimitri Donskoi* was ignored until nightfall. *Zhemchug*, near the front, was hit 17 times, but its machinery was largely undamaged. *Svyetlana* was hit two hours after the battle started, knocking out her electricity. *Vladimir Monomakh* ended up in a duel with *Izumi* early in the battle, coming off the worse. Both managed to join the cruiser line at dusk.

The auxiliaries were not as lucky as the cruisers. They wandered through the battlefield as the prey of Japanese protected cruisers and destroyers, additionally suffering the attention of the Japanese battleships when they

were otherwise unoccupied. *Ural*, an armed merchant cruiser, was supposed to be escorting the auxiliaries. A big, high-speed passenger liner armed with a set of 6in. guns, it was the first of the ships in the auxiliary line to be hit. A 12in. shell crashed into her engine room around 3.00pm. Attempting to escape, it rammed and sank *Rus*, one of two deep-sea tugs with the fleet. Crippled, *Ural* was found two hours later by *Shikishima*, and torpedoed and sunk. *Kamchatka*, the ship whose spurious sighting of Japanese torpedo boats in the North Sea nearly started a war with Britain, proved as inept at Tsushima. Straying close to the sinking *Kniaz Suvorov*, it attracted attention from nearby Japanese battleships, was shelled and sank.

Meanwhile, the surviving Russian battle line had given up attempting to lose the Japanese battle line: it was making its run to Vladivostok. By then, there were three surviving Borodino-class battleships in the 1st Division, *Sisoi Veliky*, *Navarin* and *Admiral Nakhimov* left in the 2nd Division and the almost untouched ships of Nebogatov's 3rd Division.

Over the next two hours, the Japanese ignored the 3rd Division, working their way back from the lead battleships. *Imperator Alexandr III* was the next victim of Japanese gunfire. When *Kniaz Suvorov* fell out of line, *Imperator Alexandr III* charged the Japanese battle line to distract attention from the former. As the concentrated focus of the battle line, *Imperator Alexandr III* had taken severe damage. Now, under fresh fire from the Japanese, it fell out of line at 6.30pm, swung to port and capsized. The hull sank at 7.00pm.

The Japanese next turned their guns on *Borodino*, *Oryel* and *Sisoi Veliky*. *Mikasa* and *Fuji* went for *Borodino*. *Asahi* targeted *Oryel*. *Shikishima* split its fire. *Fuji* landed a 12in. shell on *Borodino* that penetrated *Borodino*'s starboard forward 6in. turret and detonated the magazine. *Borodino* sank almost immediately; only one sailor of the 850 men aboard survived.

The only intact formation in the Russian fleet was the 3rd Division. The ancient *Imperator Nikolai I* and the three obsolete coastal defence ships in it had been sent out for the express purpose of being targets. Instead, the Japanese focused attention on the biggest prizes. The only contribution made by the 3rd Division was negative. It had fatally slowed the Pacific Fleet.

By then dusk was falling. Togo turned his battleships away from the battle line. He could resume the fight the next day. With the approaching darkness, it was time to turn over the battle to his torpedo craft and his cruisers.

TSUSHIMA: THE CONCLUSION

By the time the sun set, the Russian fleet was in the Sea of Japan, scattered around the mouth of the Tsushima Strait. The ships still operating together could not be said so much to be in formation as to be sailing in clumps.

The most important clump was made up of the survivors of the Russian battle line. It consisted of the largely untouched Third Division, *Oryel*, the damaged and sole survivor of the 1st Division and the three remaining ships of the 2nd Division: *Sisoi Veliky*, *Navarin* and *Admiral Nakhimov*. They were joined by the protected cruiser *Izumrud*, which became separated from the rest of the cruisers and tagged along with the big boys rather than spending the night alone. This group was heading north-north-east.

Another clump was formed by cruisers and destroyers. All the cruisers were present except *Almaz*, *Izumrud* and the sunken *Ural*. Six of nine destroyers were also with the cruisers. Led by Rear Admiral Enkvist, these ships were steaming south-west, heading back for the Tsushima Strait.

The smallest group was formed by the three surviving auxiliaries: supply ship *Anaduir*, tug *Svir* and ammunition ship *Koreya* (which somehow survived the day untouched). Two other auxiliaries were already sunk and *Irtuish*, which was hit at least once during the day, had broken away from the group, at dusk heading north-east. The three survivors were moving west-south-west.

Other ships wandered the battlefield in ones and twos. *Almaz* was steaming north-east, seeking to clear the battlefield. One destroyer was headed north, trying to reach Vladivostok. A pair were steaming south in company, headed to Shanghai. *Kniaz Suvorov* had been bombarded mercilessly several times by the Japanese battle line during the day as the Japanese looped around seeking the Russian battle line in the mist and smoke. Although wallowing helplessly where it had drifted to a stop, it was still afloat as night fell.

Nightfall did not end the battle. Rather, it transformed it into a disorganized, close-range brawl. At the beginning of the day, Togo sent most of his destroyers and torpedo boats to Tsushima's harbour to wait out the daylight portion of the battle. Late afternoon brought them out, to attack in the gathering darkness. Japanese ships, especially torpedo boats and destroyers, dashed in from the dark to strike the surviving Russian ships, disappeared into the gloom and then dashed in to strike again. Russian ships scattered, seeking to hide from Japanese warships that were seemingly everywhere.

Kniaz Suvorov was one of the first victims. Dead in the water, abandoned by its officers and with its guns useless, it was torpedoed by the Japanese destroyer *Murasame* and sank at 7.30pm.

The brunt of the torpedo attacks fell on the battle line, which was attacked by four destroyer divisions and one torpedo boat division. The 1st Destroyer Division was north of the Russians, then steaming north-north-east. To the north-east of the battleships

While the *Kniaz Suvorov* had been effectively knocked out of action four hours earlier, it remained afloat until dark, sinking after being torpedoed. (AC)

were the 2nd Destroyer Division and 9th Torpedo-boat Division. East of them was the 3rd Destroyer Division with the 5th Destroyer Division to their south-east.

The 3rd Destroyer Division opened the attack with a torpedo run at 8.15pm. For the next three hours they attacked the Russian line. Torpedoed during this round of attacks were the previously damaged *Sisoi Veliky* and the armoured cruiser *Admiral Nakhimov*. Both staggered out of line, crippled. *Sisoi Veliky* was hit forward and in the rudder. By 3.00am on 28 May, its bows were awash. *Admiral Nakhimov* was hit in the bow by a torpedo, reduced to a sinking condition.

The Japanese did not escape unscathed. Hits were scored on four of the destroyers and one torpedo boat making this attack.

At 2.00am, destroyers of the 4th Destroyer Division struck the Russian battle line. These ships were carrying mines in place of torpedoes. Each destroyer carried two sets of four mines, linked by a cable. Hitting the cable would bring the mines to the ship. The mines were strewn ahead of the advancing Russian vessels. The previously lightly damaged *Navarin* snagged one set of mines. Rocked by two explosions on its port bow and two explosions on its starboard bow, it capsized and sank almost immediately. Seventy men made it off the ship, but only three were later rescued.

The Russian cruisers and destroyers fared better than the Russian battle line, but not by much. As soon as the sun set, Enkvist turned his cruisers south-west and scooted through the western channel of the Tsushima Strait at top speed. Only *Aurora* and *Zhemchug* could keep up with *Oleg*, Enkvist's flagship. These three ships passed several divisions of Japanese destroyers during their flight, but went unmolested. The Japanese were hunting bigger game.

The rest of the cruiser line – *Svyetlana*, *Dmitri Donskoi* and *Vladimir Monomakh* – fell behind. Battle damage or unreliable machinery slowed. The ancient *Dmitri Donskoi* and *Vladimir Monomakh* could barely make 16

Japanese destroyers and torpedo boats tore into the surviving Russian battle line during the night. Their efforts sank one battleship, and crippled a second battleship and two armoured cruisers. (AC)

Two Japanese destroyers found the Russian destroyer *Byedovi* steaming towards Vladivostok. Aboard was an unconscious Vice Admiral Rozhestvensky. Rather than risk injuring Rozhestvensky through the strain of the chase, his chief of staff ordered the destroyer's captain to surrender. (AC)

knots on good days. *Svyetlana* was good for 21 knots, but damage brought her speed down. The Japanese 1st, 10th, 11th and 15th Torpedo-boat divisions found the cruisers while they were still in the Sea of Japan.

Svyetlana, in the lead, turned north escaping further notice from the torpedo boats. Shielded by darkness it headed towards Vladivostok. At roughly 8.40am, *Vladimir Monomakh* was approached by a torpedo boat. Mistaking it for a Russian destroyer, *Vladimir Monomakh* held fire. The Japanese warship recognized *Vladimir Monomakh* as Russian and fired its torpedoes. One hit *Vladimir Monomakh* broadside, severely damaging the old cruiser. *Vladimir Monomakh* fired back sinking the torpedo boat, probably *Number 69*. *Vladimir Monomakh* was left dead in the water. The crew laboured the rest of the night to keep it afloat.

Dmitri Donskoi fought an even more involved battle. Attacked by several waves of torpedo boats, *Dmitri Donskoi* drove all of them off. Two torpedo boats, probably *Number 74* and *Number 75* were sunk by the armoured cruiser. A third torpedo boat was seriously damaged. *Dmitri Donskoi* next beat off an attack by four protected cruisers, damaging them. Finally, losing itself in the night, *Dmitri Donskoi* crawled off to the north, heading to Vladivostok.

The Russian destroyers similarly scattered in the darkness. The 1st Destroyer Division had already separated into ones and twos that were all headed north. *Bravi*, separated from the rest, headed north as night fell. *Byedovi* and *Buini* steamed north in company, with Rozhestvensky aboard *Buini*. *Buistri* temporarily joined up with the 2nd Division, but could not keep up and decided to head for Vladivostok independently.

The 2nd Division managed to stick together for part of the night. They followed the cruisers down the western channel of the Tsushima Strait. Before they reached it, they were discovered by Japanese destroyers. *Gromki*, the fourth ship in line was torpedoed or mined, and sank. *Grozni*, bringing up the rear, lost touch with the rest of the division and headed north to Vladivostok. *Blestyashchi*, *Bezuprechni* and *Bodri* made it into the strait under cover of darkness.

Only four auxiliaries were left when darkness fell. Supply ship *Irtuish* had been hit several times during the day, become separated from the rest and ended up steaming north-east to get away from the battlefield. The other three

Almaz, built as a combination royal yacht and scout cruiser, was the only Russian warship larger than a destroyer to reach Vladivostok. It survived the Russo-Japanese War and was converted into a seaplane carrier during World War I. (AC)

– *Anadyr*, *Svir* and *Koreya* – ended the day alone and ignored. Separated from the warships assigned to guard them, they took the opportunity presented by the lack of attention from both sides and slipped out of the western channel.

Dawn found the surviving Russian fleet scattered over the Sea of Japan and Tsushima Strait. The Japanese battle line began seeking the survivors of the Russian line. By dawn, the Russian battle line had been reduced to five ships: the badly damaged *Oryel*, Nebogatov's *Imperator Nikolai I*, the absurd coastal defence ships *General Admiral Apraksin* and *Admiral Senyavin* and the cruiser *Izumrud*. They were resolutely steaming north at 7 knots, battle damage slowing the line. As with all coal-fired ships of the era, their engines produced pillars of black smoke, visible for miles.

Togo's questing cruisers soon found the Russian line, but sheered away once they made contact. By 7.00pm, Togo's battle line came over the horizon. The four battleships and two armoured cruisers of the 1st Division and the six armoured cruisers of the 2nd Division, were east and north of Nebogatov. The protected cruisers of the 4th and 6th divisions were south of him.

By 9.00am, Nebogatov's small force was surrounded. The Japanese battleships began shelling the Russians from 12,000 yards. The maximum range of the Russian guns was 11,000 yards and the surviving ships were low on ammunition. Nebogatov could not run. The Japanese could go half-again as fast as his best speed. He could not hide: the day was clear. He could not fight: the Japanese outnumbered him. Nebogatov ordered his fleet to surrender rather than see his men slaughtered. He believed he would be court-martialled and shot for this decision, but if he fought on he would die anyway. Surrender ensured no one else other than he himself would die.

It took a while to convince the Japanese he was surrendering. He finally had his ships stop dead in the water and raised tablecloths as white flags before the Japanese finally understood his intention. Within the Russian warships there was resistance. Rather than stop, *Izumrud* rehoisted its flags, went to full speed and steamed north, pursued by Togo's cruisers. *Izumrud* outraced them escaping surrender. The Japanese had no sooner secured their prizes than they saw smoke to the south. The armoured cruisers *Iwate* and *Tokawa* were sent to investigate. It was from *Admiral Ushakov*, the third coastal defence ship, which had become separated during the night. When *Admiral Ushakov* ignored a signal to surrender, the cruisers opened fired.

Soon joined by the rest of the 2nd Division, they battered *Admiral Ushakov*. Its crew opened the seacocks, scuttling the ship rather than surrendering.

The rest of the day proceeded in the same fashion, with Japanese ships hunting down Russian survivors. Two Japanese cruisers found *Svyetlana* off the Korean coast and sank the combination yacht-cruiser. *Gromski* was chased down by Japanese destroyers and sunk. *Bistri*, caught by other Japanese light warships, ran aground on the Korean coast.

Three crippled vessels littered the water north-east of the Tsushima Islands. Battleship *Sisoi Veliky* and armoured cruisers *Admiral Nakhimov* and *Vladimir Monomakh*, all torpedoed during the night action, were drifting south-east, unable to move at more than a crawl. When Japanese warships appeared on the horizon, the cruisers were scuttled to prevent capture. *Sisoi Veliky* surrendered, but sank before the Japanese could take possession.

Irtuish found itself alone on the Sea of Japan. It had fled east. Badly damaged during the previous day, it was run aground off Mishima Island to prevent capture by the Japanese cruiser *Izumi*.

Three other Russian warships were caught in the vicinity of Ulleung Island (today's Ulleung-gun). *Dimitri Donski*, in a sinking condition, anchored near the island, transferring its crew ashore before finally going under. The destroyers *Buini* and *Byedovi* were headed to Vladivostok when *Buini*'s engines quit. Its crew, the survivors it picked up the previous day and the unconscious Rozhestvensky were transferred to *Byedovi*. As it steamed north, it was spotted by two Japanese destroyers. Worried about the effects of a high-speed chase on his wounded leader, Rozhestvensky's chief of staff ordered the captain of the overloaded *Byedovi* to surrender. The surprised commander of the Japanese forces discovered he had captured the Russian fleet commander. Rozhestvensky was transferred to a naval hospital in Japan.

Some Russian ships escaped. Only three – *Almaz*, *Bravi* and *Grozni* – made it to Vladivostok. *Izumrud* eventually reached the Siberian coast, but a navigation error put her far from Vladivostok. Badly damaged and low on fuel, its captain beached the cruiser. Its crew reached Vladivostok overland.

Of the three 2nd Division destroyers that made it through the Tsushima Strait, one, *Bezuprechni*, sank due to battle damage in the strait. *Blestyashchi* ran out of fuel after exiting the strait. By then it was daylight, and *Blestyashchi* was in company with *Bodri*. The latter stopped, picked up *Blestyashchi*'s crew and eventually reached Shanghai. The three cruisers led by Enkvist made it to the Philippines, and slipped into Manila and internment.

Anaduir, *Svir* and *Koreya* also reached safety. *Svir* and *Koreya* straggled into Shanghai separately, but *Anaduir* seemingly disappeared. Initially, it was reported sunk during the battle. Since *Svir* and *Koreya* both saw the transport enter the Yellow Sea on the 28th, this was discounted. Nothing further was heard of *Anaduir* immediately after the battle; it was believed the ship had sunk due to battle damage, especially since the Japanese reported sinking it during the battle. Possibly it was only damaged but succumbed later.

The mystery was resolved one month later, when *Anaduir* steamed into port at Madagascar. Avoiding detection, capture and internment, it retraced its path and was attempting to head home, the last ship of either side to reach harbour after Tsushima.

Rozhestvensky was hurried to a naval hospital as soon as he arrived in Japan. Although a prisoner, he was treated as an honoured guest. Togo visited Rozhestvensky when the latter was recovering, to show respect for a determined and honourable foe. (AC)

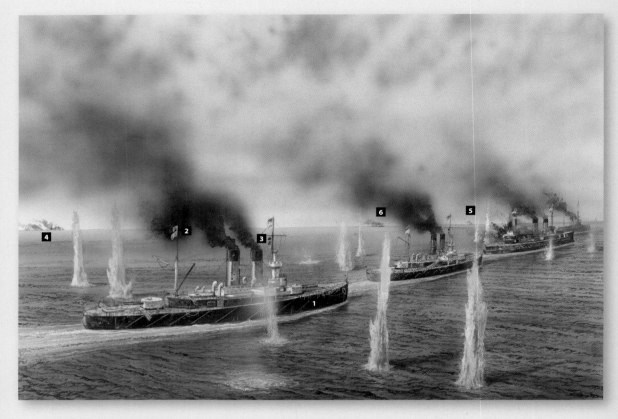

THE SURRENDER OF THE RUSSIAN FLEET AT TSUSHIMA (PP. 86–87)

Once Admiral Nebogatov had ordered a surrender, the issue of how to let their opponent know remained. Ship-to-ship radio was in its infancy in 1905. A radio message to the Japanese could not be made, leaving signal flags and searchlight semaphore.

At first, Nebogatov had his ships lower the Russian national and naval flags. He also had them raise phonetic flags signaling 'X', 'G', 'E'. Striking colours was a traditional way of signalling surrender. Nebogatov was reinforcing it with the XGE signal. XGE in the maritime International Code of Signals then used meant 'I surrender'. By the time of Tsushima, having flags shot away during battle was common, so the Japanese were unaware the Russian flags were lowered deliberately, rather than unintentionally shot away due to combat damage.

The Imperial Japanese Navy used its own signal book, which did not list XGE as meaning 'I surrender'. Indeed, the IJN codebook lacked any signal for surrendering. It took time to find a copy of the International Code of Signals and translate the message to Japanese. Togo's battleship continued firing at the Russians. At this point *Izumrud* lowered the XGE signal, raised its ensigns and pulled out of the battle line. At flank speed it headed south, away from the Japanese battleships. It set course north after discovering Uryu's cruisers south of it. With its boilers set full,

it soon reached its top speed of 24 knots – or maybe exceeded that and disappeared over the horizon with Japanese cruisers in pursuit.

Frustrated at the lack of response, Nebogatov ordered white tablecloths raised in place of the naval ensigns. A white flag was a positive signal of surrender. Unfortunately, during the Sino-Japanese War a Chinese warship had tricked Togo, using a white flag to escape from the cruiser Togo then commanded. Togo ordered the white flags ignored and his ships continued to fire.

Nebogatov then ordered Japanese naval ensigns hoisted over the white flags and had his ships stop engines. The sight of the Japanese flags through the rangefinders of the warships firing on the Russian ship was reported to Togo on the bridge of the *Mikasa*. Finally understanding the significance of the Russian actions, Togo ordered a ceasefire.

This plate shows the scene a few moments after the Japanese ceased firing on Nebogatov's squadron. The Russian ships (**1**) are dead in the water, with their engines stopped. The flags and tablecloths can be seen at the mast tops (**2**) and the XGE signal flying from the signal halyards (**3**). Behind the Russian ships, Togo's battleships can be seen (**4**). *Izumrud*'s smoke (**5**) can be seen in the distance along with that of the pursuing Japanese cruisers (**6**).

AFTERMATH

Togo had won the most decisive major naval battle of the 20th century. Even the massive naval actions of the Pacific War 40 years later would not produce a victory on the same scale with such lopsided results: the Battle of the Java Sea may have been as one-sided as Tsushima, but it was on a smaller scale, while the Battle of Leyte was a larger engagement than Tsushima, but the majority of the defeated fleet survived to fight again and the victors lost several significant warships.

The Russo-Japanese War did not end with the Battle of Tsushima any more than the earlier and equally decisive land battle of Mukden brought things to a conclusion. Japan was incapable of physically defeating Russia. If Russia was willing to fight, the war would continue. Even after Tsushima, even with a revolution convulsing Russia, Tsar Nicholas was still unwilling to concede defeat.

Japan was running out of manpower and money. Although Russia was unaware of it, Japan could not continue the war much longer, even after Tsushima. In February 1905, President Theodore Roosevelt of the United States offered to mediate peace between Russia and Japan. Japan was willing, but Russia was not. At Roosevelt's suggestion, Japan invaded Sakhalin Island in July, then repositioned its ground forces to invade Vladivostok.

The bluff brought Russia to the bargaining table. Meeting at Portsmouth, New Hampshire, a peace agreement was hammered out after 12 sessions. Russia paid no reparations but conceded the Liaodong Peninsula and half of Sakhalin Island to Japan, and removed all its military forces from Manchuria. Korea became a Japanese protectorate.

The peace treaty was met with relief in Russia and riots in Japan. Unaware of Japan's weaknesses and convinced of Japanese invincibility, Japan's people saw the Portsmouth Treaty as humiliating.

Rozhestvensky recovered from his injuries. He was repatriated to Russia along with Nebogatov and the other captured officers and men of the Imperial Russian Navy at the war's end. Rozhestvensky, Nebogatov and other senior officers (including the chief of staff who ordered *Byedovi*'s surrender) were court-martialled. Rozhestvensky pled guilty, assuming

Peace talks were held at Portsmouth, New Hampshire, USA, then a summer resort for the wealthy. The reputation led to suggestions, as illustrated by this political cartoon, that the remaining issues could be settled through sports competitions. (LOC)

The aftermath of Tsushima.

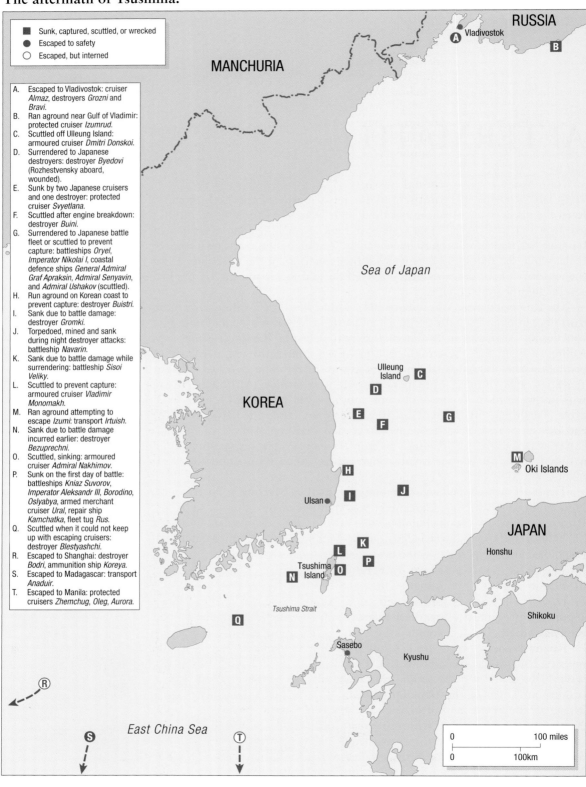

- ■ Sunk, captured, scuttled, or wrecked
- ● Escaped to safety
- ○ Escaped, but interned

A. Escaped to Vladivostok: cruiser *Almaz*, destroyers *Grozni* and *Bravi*.
B. Ran aground near Gulf of Vladimir: protected cruiser *Izumrud*.
C. Scuttled off Ulleung Island: armoured cruiser *Dmitri Donskoi*.
D. Surrendered to Japanese destroyers: destroyer *Byedovi* (Rozhestvensky aboard, wounded).
E. Sunk by two Japanese cruisers and one destroyer: protected cruiser *Svyetlana*.
F. Scuttled after engine breakdown: destroyer *Buini*.
G. Surrendered to Japanese battle fleet or scuttled to prevent capture: battleships *Oryel*, *Imperator Nikolai I*, coastal defence ships *General Admiral Graf Apraksin*, *Admiral Senyavin*, and *Admiral Ushakov* (scuttled).
H. Run aground on Korean coast to prevent capture: destroyer *Buistri*.
I. Sank due to battle damage: destroyer *Gromki*.
J. Torpedoed, mined and sank during night destroyer attacks: battleship *Navarin*.
K. Sank due to battle damage while surrendering: battleship *Sisoi Veliky*.
L. Scuttled to prevent capture: armoured cruiser *Vladimir Monomakh*.
M. Ran aground attempting to escape *Izumi*: transport *Irtuish*.
N. Sank due to battle damage incurred earlier: destroyer *Bezuprechni*.
O. Scuttled, sinking: armoured cruiser *Admiral Nakhimov*.
P. Sunk on the first day of battle: battleships *Kniaz Suvorov*, *Imperator Aleksandr III*, *Borodino*, *Oslyabya*, armed merchant cruiser *Ural*, repair ship *Kamchatka*, fleet tug *Rus*.
Q. Scuttled when it could not keep up with escaping cruisers: destroyer *Blestyashchi*.
R. Escaped to Shanghai: destroyer *Bodri*, ammunition ship *Koreya*.
S. Escaped to Madagascar: transport *Anaduir*.
T. Escaped to Manila: protected cruisers *Zhemchug*, *Oleg*, *Aurora*.

RUSSIA

Vladivostok

MANCHURIA

Sea of Japan

KOREA

Ulleung Island

Ulsan

Tsushima Island

Tsushima Strait

Sasebo

JAPAN

Honshu

Oki Islands

Shikoku

Kyushu

East China Sea

| 0 | | 100 miles |
| 0 | | 100km |

responsibility for the loss although he was wounded and unconscious for most of the battle. He was pardoned and retired.

Nebogatov and the others associated with the surrender were sentenced to death. These were commuted to prison sentences by Tsar Nicholas, in part because Rozhestvensky assumed responsibility for the battle's outcome at his trial. It was difficult to shoot the subordinates when their commander had been pardoned.

Togo became a national hero. Venerated within Japan and hailed as Nelson's successor in the rest of the world, he was the symbol of the Imperial Japanese Navy until his death in 1934.

Battleship main guns did most of the damage during the naval battles of the Russo-Japanese War. This led to the design of a new type of battleship with more main battery guns and no secondary battery. The result was HMS *Dreadnought*, relegating all older battleships to the category of 'pre-Dreadnought battleships'. (USNHHC)

The Imperial Russian Navy never recovered from the war. In 18 months, it went from the world's third largest navy to the seventh largest. Its post-war Pacific Fleet consisted mainly of the ships which escaped to Vladivostok or internment. It rebuilt, but World War I and the October Revolution put paid to its plans.

Japan not only gained a place on the world stage, it increased its navy. After the war, it raised virtually every Russian warship sunk in Japanese-controlled ports, repaired them and added them with the ships captured at Tsushima to the Imperial Japanese Navy. By 1906, Japan's navy had more than doubled in size.

Largely as a result of Tsushima, Britain developed a new type of battleship. At Tsushima, the damage was done mainly by battleships' main batteries. Secondary batteries proved ineffective or a distraction. Britain's new battleship omitted secondary batteries, and in their place, additional 12in. turrets were added. This new ship, HMS *Dreadnought*, had ten 12in. guns in five twin turrets. Its broadside of eight 12in. guns was the equivalent of the firepower of two traditional battleships.

Dreadnought, commissioned in 1906, gave its name to the new class of warship. All previous battleships, which now became known as pre-Dreadnought battleships, were obsolete overnight. All navies, including Japan and Russia, had to start over. Japan's prizes were re-rated as coastal defence ships.

Japan drew two false lessons from the Russo-Japanese War and ignored a real one. It concluded that beating the biggest bully in the neighbourhood allowed you to replace that bully. Having defeated a Russia bullying its Asian neighbours for the past 50 years, Japan replaced Russia as the neighbourhood bully. It missed the lesson that bullies (like Russia and later Japan) invite their own eventual defeat. Japan also quickly forgot how close it came to defeat, ignoring the lucky breaks granted by fortune and the quiet assistance it received from the United States and Britain. As a result, Japan concluded victory resulted from stubborn tenacity.

These conceits proved fatal in the 1940s. Japan picked a fight with a nation bigger and more powerful than itself, after alienating all potential allies, and it lost.

THE BATTLEFIELD TODAY

The grey waters of the Tsushima Strait and the Sea of Japan remain heavily travelled today. Shipping going to and from Japan or Siberia crosses its length, and ferries between Korea and Japan cross its breadth. Most are diesel-powered motor ships rather than the coal-fired steamers of 1904–05.

The various ships wrecked on the coastlines involved in the Russo-Japanese War were either salvaged in the years immediately after the war or scrapped in place. Port Arthur is known as Lüshunkou District today. It has been overtaken in size by the other port on the Liaodong Peninsula, Dalian (formerly Dalny). Traces of the Russian fortifications and harbour facilities remain visible at Lüshunkou today.

Below the surface of the Yellow Sea, Sea of Japan and Tsushima Strait visible relics of the war can still be seen today. The sea bottom is littered

When retired, *Mikasa* was converted to a museum ship. It can be visited today at Yokohama, Japan. (SDASM)

92

with wrecks from ships sunk during the conflict. The waters make these challenging dive targets, although ships in the shallower Yellow Sea are frequently visited, especially those sunk off the Liaodong Peninsula. A few have been salvaged, most notably the *Admiral Nakhimov*. A Japanese businessman sponsored a dive in 1980 that recovered gold, platinum and British sovereigns. One of *Nakhimov*'s guns was also recovered and is on display at the Museum of Maritime Science in Tokyo.

Two ships that fought in the battle still exist as museum ships, one from each side: the battleship *Mikasa* and the cruiser *Aurora*.

Mikasa is to Japan what HMS *Victory* is to Britain or USS *Constitution* is to the United States: a ship symbolic of a nation's maritime heritage. After *Mikasa* was almost destroyed in a magazine explosion in 1905, it was rebuilt. In 1922, obsolete but still cherished, it was decommissioned in 1922 and turned into a museum ship. Badly neglected during the 1940s, it was restored in the late 1950s. Instrumental in raising funds was Admiral Chester Nimitz, who helped defeat Japan in World War II, but deeply admired Togo. The ship, with its hull encased in concrete, can be visited today.

Although *Aurora* played only a minor part in the Battle of Tsushima, it was similarly preserved. It returned to the Baltic in 1906 after release from internment in Manila. It served as a cadet training ship from 1906 to 1912. After service in World War I, it returned to Petrograd (St Petersburg) for a refit. While there it fired the first shot of the 1917 October Revolution. After hard service in the Russian Revolution and World War II, *Aurora* was restored as a museum ship. While originally preserved as a symbol of the Soviet Union, it is now kept for its overall cultural and historical importance, including its service in the Imperial Russian Navy. Now moored in St Petersburg, it is open to the public.

FURTHER READING

There is no war as obscure today about which more has been written than the Russo-Japanese War of 1904–05. It was the first large war of the 20th century. Publishers made a minor industry of turning out accounts of the war between 1904 when it started and 1914 when a newer, larger war dissipated interest in the Russo-Japanese War.

A wealth of information is available about the men, the ships and the battles from books written during this period. Some treat the war as if it were a sporting event. Others are sober analyses, seeking to extract insight from the results. Many were written by participants on both sides and naval experts of the era.

Some books must be read carefully. Nikolai Klado was a major advocate of the disastrous decision to send a 3rd Pacific Squadron. His first book contains the articles that led the Russian Admiralty to send reinforcements. His second (written after Tsushima) explains why sending the ships was the right decision, if only Rozhestvensky had used them properly. (Experts like Klado are never wrong – in their minds.) Yet useful information can be extracted from both.

Twenty-five years ago these sources were available only at research libraries through interlibrary loan. Today many are online, available through

Aurora survived the Russo-Japanese War, World War I, World War II, and the Cold War. Originally preserved due to her role in the Russian Revolution, *Aurora* remains a symbol of Russia's naval heritage, and can be visited today in St Petersburg. (Dennis G. Jarvis)

repositories like archive.org or Google Books. These are marked with an asterisk in the selection that follows, which lists some of the works consulted for this book.

Brassey, T. A. (ed.), *The Naval Annual, 1903*, J. Griffin and Co., Portsmouth, 1903*
——, *The Naval Annual, 1906*, J. Griffin and Co., Portsmouth, 1906*
Cassell's History of the Russo-Japanese War (5 Volumes), Cassell and Company, Limited, London, Paris, New York and Melbourne, 1905*
Connaughton, R. M., *War of the Rising Sun and Tumbling Bear: A Military History of the Russo-Japanese War, 1904–5*, Routledge, London and New York, 1988
The Historical Section of the Committee of Imperial Defence, *Official History (Naval and Military) of the Russo-Japanese War (In Three Volumes)*, HMSO/Harrison and Sons, London, 1908, 1910, 1920*
Hough, Richard, *The Fleet that Had to Die*, Hamish Hamilton Ltd, London, 1958
Jane, Fred T., *The Imperial Russian Navy: Its Past, Present and Future*, W. Thacker & Co., London, 1899*
——, *The Imperial Japanese Navy*, W. Thacker & Co., London, 1904*
Klado, Nicolas, *The Battle of the Sea of Japan*, Hurst and Blackett Ltd., London, 1906*
——, *The Russian Navy in the Russo-Japanese War*, Hurst and Blackett Ltd., London, 1905*
Kowner, Rotem, *The A to Z of the Russo-Japanese War*, The Scarecrow Press Inc., Lanham, MD, 2009
Seppings Wright, H. C., *With Togo: The Story of Seven Months Active Service under his Command*, Hurst and Blackett Ltd, London, 1907*
Steer, A. P., *The 'Novik' and the Part she Played in the Russo-Japanese War, 1904*, John Murray, London, 1913*
Tikowara Hesibo (trans. Grant, Robert), *Before Port Arthur in a Destroyer: The Personal Diary of a Japanese Naval Officer*, E. P. Dutton and Co., New York, 1907*
Togo Kichitaro, *The Naval Battles of the Russo-Japanese War*, Gogakukyokwai, Tokyo, 1907*

INDEX